The Genesis Of Writing

HIEROGLYPHICS

By Kwasi Milton

UNITED BROTHERS COMMUNICATIONS SYSTEM
1040 Settlers Landing Road Suite D
Hampton, Virginia 23669
(804) 723-2696

FIRST EDITION ● FIRST PRINTING

FEBRUARY, 1992

Copyright 1992 (C) By Kwasi Milton. No part of this book may be reproduced or copied without the expressed, written permission of the publisher. UBCS; 1040 Settlers Landing Road Suite D, Hampton, Virginia 23669.

ISBN# 1-56411-018-4   Y.B.B.G.# 0020

PRINTED IN THE U. S. A. By
United Brother Graphics and Printing Company
1040 Settlers Landing Road Suite D
Hampton, Virginia 23669
(804) 723-2696

Contents

Hieroglyphics and the Art of Writing	1
Coptic	45
Coptic and the Hieroglyphics	61
Greek Philosophy	72
Hieroglyphics and Biblical Creation in Genesis	78
Conclusion	89
Appendix	97

This book is dedicated to everybody

with an African ancestry---

the whole human race !

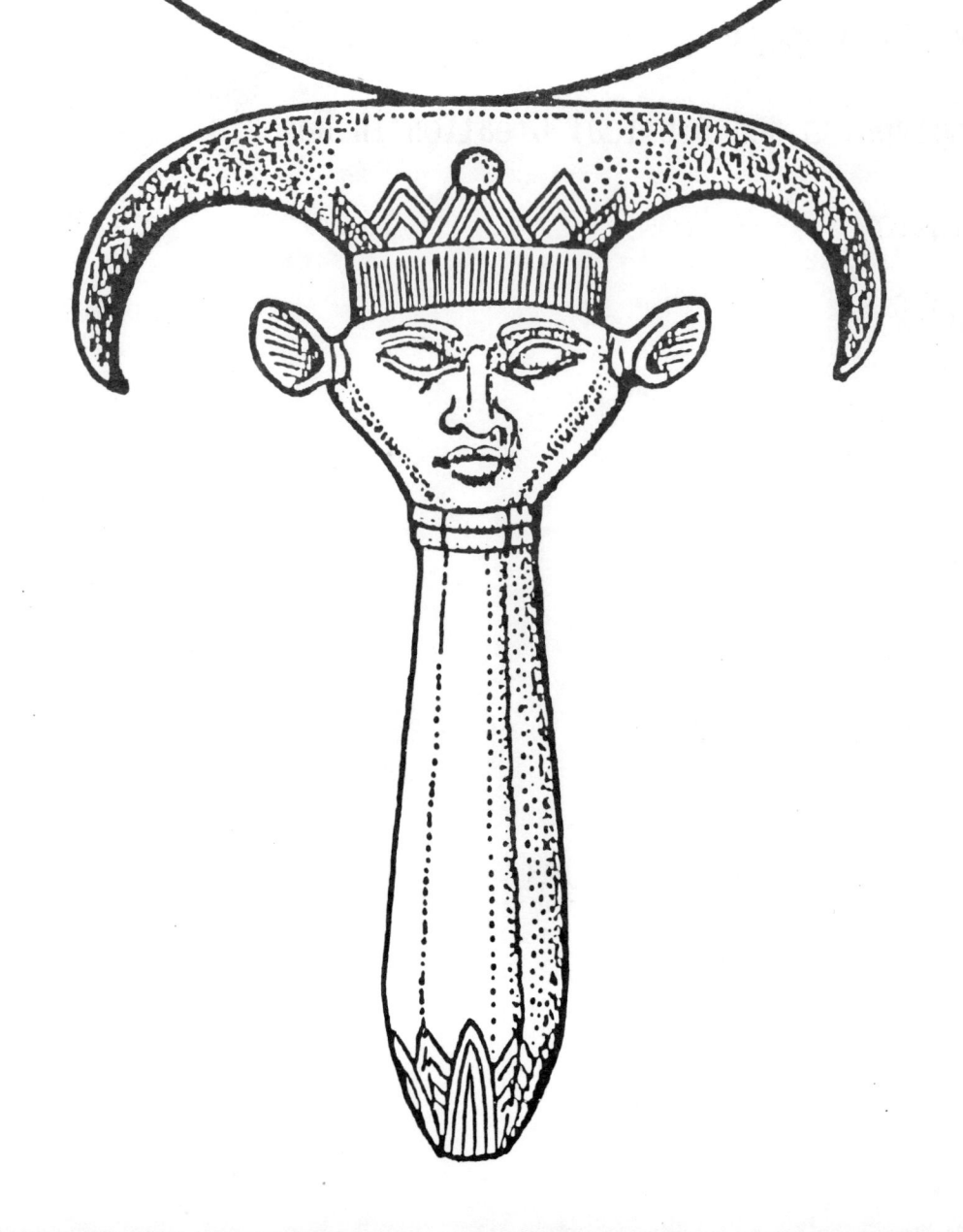

INTRODUCTION

This publication is itself an introduction to the hieroglyphics. The authors' intent is to simplify a complicated subject, and to create some interest for many not acquainted with the hieroglyphics.

Writing, and reading for that matter, are taken for granted. All that has been achieved by the human animal today was made possible by the art of writing. The wealth of science and technology developed over the course of human history required a vehicle to pass it on from generation to generation, and culture to culture, else the human animal would have been stagnated re-learning the same things from generation to generation, and not progressing to higher learning.

Etched in stone, the hieroglyphics remain available for study. Ancient during the time it was used in Egypt, this writing is the earliest point that we can trace human transcription. Oddly enough, our modern script can be linked to the hieroglyphics by way of the Coptic.

The ancient Greeks greatly appreciated what they learned from the Egyptians, and their almost carbon copy of the Coptic alphabet was passed on to the western world. Writing helped the human animal communicate with its family components. The advent of the art of writing facilitated the first step toward the mastery of the elements and exploration of our beautiful garden called earth.

Although the ethnic background of the ancient Egyptians is well documented, its not so widely known. The prelude to understanding the motivation behind the development of Egyptian writing, the precursor of modern western writing, is the understanding of the culture that gave it birth.

The African origin of the Egyptians is reiterated throughout this publication to keep the reader focused. Examples of both the hieroglyphics and the Coptic scripts are given with modern translations. The decorative graphics employed were obtained from Dover Publications, *"Ancient Egyptians, for artist and craft people"* by Eva Wilson and *"Ancient Egyptian Design, coloring book"* by Ed Sibbett Jr.

--- THE AUTHOR

ABOUT THE AUTHOR

I grew up in the city of New York, and have lived there for 37 years, moving to Florida in 1988. After spending two (2) years at the Borough of Manhattan Community College, I transferred to the City College of New York where I received my Bachelor of Science degree in 1976.

While at Manhattan Community College I received a cultural exchange scholarship, along with 50 other African American students, to the Ghana. this was the first of several cultural exchange groups of its kind. We remained in Africa for one month, staying at the University of Ghana. Later the group went to Nigeria for a period of one week.

In 1971 I was introduced to the "Egyptian Book of the Dead" by E.A.W Budge and "Problems In African History" by Robert Collins. Immediately, it became apparent that there existed an ancient African literary world almost unexplored by African Americans, whose upward mobilization could be motivated by the simple realization of its existence as a integral part of their history.

Before I realized it, the ancient ancestors had seized control of my being, and I was hopelessly addicted to the study and research of the hieroglyphics. This study guided me to the Coptic language. The more I researched old out of print material the more I uncovered, and realized the vast amount of material that needed to be re-examined. Thinking that the task was to great for myself, I was content that aware African American scholars would come forward and answer the calling. Most of the materials I found written by African American scholars only scratched the surface or crammed so much general information together so as to further confuse and overwhelm the African American reading masses. All too often I've found material on the subject impregnated with Black emotionalism and sheer speculation, so as to take the universal credit away from the African science of Egyptology and the linguistical study of it. At any rate the ancient African voices of the past remain very much alive within the vast literature left behind. Motivated by the echo of those voices, I find that I, as many others, are placed in the position of either heeding the call or betray it. Many have choosen the former. I am counted among them. Therefore my manuscript "Hieroglyphics the Genesis of Writing" is the first of a series of manuscripts I plan to produce. Contained in this manuscript are some very innovative materials. I consider this work a primer on the subject. The hieroglyphics used in this production were very carefully choosen, and the translations are very literal, using the current knowledge of the hieroglyphics, coupled with logical deduction. The derivation of the words "Egypt" and "Coptic" are unique to this manuscript. Using etymology and logical deduction based on established facts, I have convincingly demonstrated the African origin of both words from the same root word. I am confident that my dedication to this work, and my relentless research will prove itself in the quality of the manuscript.

Independantly, I've studied the Coptic language. In particular, the Coptic language is the oldest written African language on earth, and in general it is the oldest written language in the world. There is no language on earth that has such an extensive written history. An understanding of the hieroglyphics grammar necessitates a rudimentry knowledge of Coptic. As a classical African language, Coptic is to the African world what Latin became for the western world. A search for an African scholastic language in my judgment ends with the Coptic. It alone connects Africa to world civilization and culture. Often one will find a simple statement interjected when ever reference is made about the Coptic alphabet, that it is derived from the Greek with the addition of 7 letters. This single statement by modern western scholars attempts to conceal the fact that the Greek alphabet was derived from the Egyptians, and it leads one to believe that the Coptic is merely a inferior copy of the Greek. This may explain why many African American scholars failed to realize the importance of the Coptic language. It is my mission to clear up the misconception regarding this language, and to revive it. Currently, I have two Coptic manuscripts ready for publication.

Through linguistics I've tackled the study of the hieroglyphics and the ancient civilizations of the Nile valley. The fact that the Coptic language is descendant from the official language of the ancient Egyptians, and it has changed very little from its early beginnings, save for only dialects, makes it a valuable tool to linguistically examine the language of the hieroglyphics. Contrary to western speculation, the Coptic language greatly influeneced the Greek language. This is to say, many words found in ancient Greek were merely Egyptian words that were Greek-ized. Ancient writers such as Herodotus and Deodorus Siculus clearly indicate that prior to the arrival of Africans who colonized a portion of Greece and set of the Greek city of Thebes (after the African city of the same name), the Greeks had no written language. They further explain that these Africans introduced writing to the Greeks. It would stand to logical reason that this early contact with Africans would have some affect on the Greek language. Thus by the time that Alexander the Great's armies arrived in Egypt, the Greek language was already mixed with a large number of African words to such a degree that it was sometimes difficult to distinguish which words were of Greek origin or borrowed from the Egyptians. In these cases, western scholars have arbitrarily claimed these words for the Greeks. My purpose is the restoration and the radiation of the literature from classical African civilizations through linguistics, for contained within it is the genesis of the kingdom both within and without.

ⲦⲘⲈⲚⲦⲈⲢⲞ ⲚⲀϤⲢⲒⲔⲁ ⲤⲈⲘⲠⲈⲦⲈⲚϨⲞⲨⲚ ⲀⲨⲰ ⲤⲈⲘⲠⲈⲦⲈⲚⲂⲁⲗ

Sincerely

Kwasi

Civilizations Prelude

The intense heat blazing like a fire ball, and stemming from the combustion of specially developed fuel, pushing against the earth's surface, propelling the United States' shuttle in space, is reminiscent of a discription in the ancient book of "Enoch", telling of a fire powered chariot. This historical launching was achieved through the utilization of all the knowledge accumulated by the human specie to date and was another great step forward for humanity. This coordinated effort, combinding and integrating aquired knowledge is one of the marks of civilization.

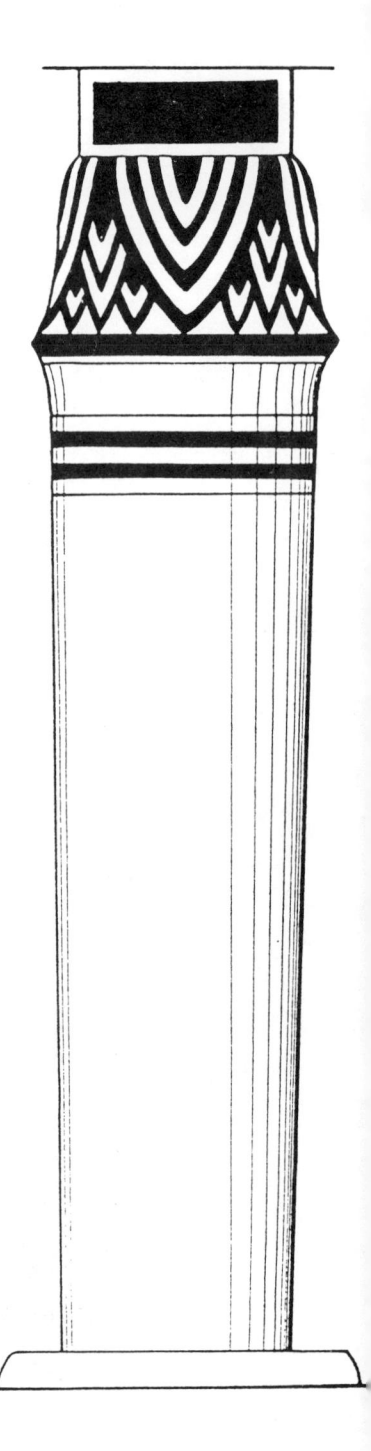

For our purpose here, let us say that civilization is a literate culture. A civilized society contains scholars and scientists. Scholars consolidate and clarify acquired knowledge. This knowledge is expanded by scientists, who experiment on it, for further practical applications. The consolidation and clarification of human knowledge gained from historical experiences, must be recorded, in order for it to serve as a reference for future applications. Both scholars and scientist depend on the transcription of the knowledge acquired by the human brain. Written word is one of the voices of the brain that expresses the minds historical experiences. Scholars and scientists are vital to civilizations, whom in turn require the written word. The art of writing is therefore, a prerequisite for a civilized society.

The ancient ancestors of humanity passed down the expanded acquired knowledge through the art of writing, along with the art itself. These ancestors were our chosen ones. They are the foundation of our modern civilized societies. Let's begin with the period in human history after the advent of writing, the period of its transmission. This point in history is known as the dynastic period of ancient Egypt. Ancient Egyptian society was built upon the acquired knowledge of the Nile Valley Civilizations.

Much has been written and said about the Ancient Egyptians. For many, Egypt is a baffling phenomenon. Certainly it is impressive, with its mighty monuments, and its reputation for vast learning and skills. She was and is a shining emblem of the creative motivation of the human spirit expressed through the development of society and culture. Its civilization flourished for such a long period of time that it was ancient, even to the ancients.

Ancient Egypt as part and parcel to the Nile Valley Civilizations, is the cradle of our modern high-tech society. Without her initial contributions, many of the conveniences enjoyed in our world of today would not be possible. She represent the earliest starting point from which world culture and civilization can be traced.

Several Egyptologist have theorized that the ancient Egyptians originally came from Asia. This theory, however, cannot be substanciated with any meaningful data. At one time this thesis was fashionable to entertain, only because scholars were seeking some sensational mystery about a people who attained a high level of development in very ancient times. They cannot be faulted for their early theories, as the development of ancient Egypt was so magnificant and almost impossible to believe, that anyone might be tempted to even suggest aliens from another planet were responsible. Much of our present education attempts to dress the ancient world in the new world's clothes, and remold the old images in the likeness of the new ones. If we asked ourselves; who were the ancient Egyptians, as an ethnic group ? What answer would our modern education provide us with ? Some may feel that it does not merit an answer. Ancient Egyptian culture and history is the heritage of the Human Race. Were it not for the changing of the old with the new, the inquiry would not exist in the first place. At any rate we will take this inquiry to conclusion.

Let us begin our inquiry, with the dead. The ancient Greeks, the precursors of western civilization, left many writings behind, as revelations of the world's past. Colchida, mentioned in Greek mythology, is also a real location, at the foot of the Caucasian Mountains, on the Black Sea. Mount Ararat, where an ark alleged to belong to the Biblical Noah was found, is also located in this area. The site of ancient Colchida is now within the territory of the U.S.S.R, and is known as the Abkhazian Autonomous Soviet Socialist Republic. It has such a large black population that it's called the "Black Soviet". The ancient Greek scholar

Herodotus, has quite an interesting story to tell us about the black people of Colchida. Let us awaken him from the dead and conduct a conversation with him through our special historical "Medium".

MEDIUM: Herodotus, called the Greek father of history, believed to have lived 484 to 424 B.C., and compiled from ancient sources, a nine volume work called "History". Speak with us today, and in your own words tell us what you know about the people of Colchida

HERODOTUS: "..It is undoubtably a fact that the Colchians are of Egyptian descent."

MEDIUM: Are you certain ? On what grounds do you base your answer regarding this matter?

HERODOTUS: "..My own idea on the matter is based on the fact that they have black skin and crinkly hair. I asked questions in both Colchida and Egypt, and found that the Colchians remembered the Egyptians, more distinctly than the Egyptians remembered them. The Egyptians did, however, say that they thought the early Colcians were from Sesostris' army."
(Ramses II, Herodotus p167 Penguin Press, 1972)

MEDIUM: Diodorus, Greek historian of the first century compiler of many books, what have you to say about the Egyptians?

DIODORUS: " The Ethiopians, say that Egypt is one of their colonies. They add that it is from them (Ethiopians) that they (Egyptians) learned to honor their kings as gods and bury their dead with such pomp. Sculpture and writing were born in the land of Ethiopia. "

The Egyptians and Ethiopians were kin to each other. The fame of ancient Ethiopia was world wide, and Herodotus and others spoke very highly of them. Herodotus described the Ethiopians as the tallest, most beautiful, and long lived of the human race. Others, in more flattering language, spoke of them as the most just of men, and favorite of the gods.

There is an interesting account of a episode between a Persian king named Chambises (Khambises), who after taking Egypt, cast his eyes on Ethiopia. History, state that this Persian king was a madman, and this may very well have been the case, for to attempt to subdue Ethiopia at this time in history, was truly madness. The Persian king sent spies to Ethiopia with scarlet robes and gold chain necklaces, palm wine and myrrh. It seems that the wise soothsayers of Ethiopia must have warned the king, for his reply to the spies was thus;

" The king of Persia has not sent you with these presents because he puts a high value on being my friend. You have come to get information about my kingdom. Therefore you are liars and that king of yours is a wicked man. Had he any respect for what is right, he would have not coveted any kingdom other than his own, nor made slaves of a people who have done him no ill.

So take him this bow (the Ethiopian bow was six feet long), and tell him the king of Ethiopia has some advice for him. When the Persians can draw a bow of this size thus easily, then let him raise an army of superior strength and invade the country of the long lived Ethiopians. Until then, let him thank the gods (orishas) for not turning the thought of the children of Ethiopia to foreign conquest. "

Of course the Persian king was furious, but he nor any of his troops could draw an Ethiopian bow. His attempts to invade Ethiopia failed. He met his death after violating ancient Egyptian sacred rites, including inflicting a sword wound to the thigh of a sacred cow, causing the death of the animal. He met with the same fate, while riding his chariot, his own sword cut into his thigh, complications developed and he later died of gangrene.

Lets continue our conversation with the dead. This time we'll speak with the late Keeper of the Egyptian and Assyrian Antiquities, British Museum, Sir E.A Wallis Budge, born 1857 and died November 23, 1934.

MEDIUM: You've published many books on Egypt, and in your first publication, the "MUMMY", you said that the Egyptians were Caucasians. Perhaps you would like to elaborate on your statement, in view of the fact that ancient Greek scholars who were in contact with the Egyptians, differ with you.

BUDGE: "the very small attention that I have been able to devote to the grammar and vocabulary of some of the peoples languages now spoken in the eastern Sudan has convinced me that they contain much that is useful for the study of the language of the hieroglyphics. The ancient Egyptians were African people and they spoke an African language. The people of modern Sudan are Africans and they speak African languages."

MEDIUM: We see that you have changed your position. It seems that you found some clues in the study of the Egyptian language.

BUDGE: "A very large number of words found in the Egyptian language are monosyllabic and were invented by the oldest African people in the valley of the Nile. The primitive home of the people who invented these words lay far to the south of Egypt, in the Great Lakes region (Nyanza Lakes), toward the east of them."
(Budge, LXVIII, Egyptian Hieroglyphic Dictionary, vol I Dover Press)

Nothing can be said of the ancient Egyptians without mention of the Ethiopians. Deodorus tells us that the Ethiopians claim that the Egypt was a Ethiopian colony. This claim is not unreasonable. For the most part, the Ethiopians and the Egyptians were a black skinned people, who lived in a close proximity to each other. Scholars have already traced the origin of humanity to the continent of Africa. This should be of no real surprise. The book of Genesis in the Old Testament of the Bible creates a scenario of the Garden of Eden, that suggest a location in South East Africa. Genesis 2:8 read "And the Lord God planted a garden eastward in Eden and there He put the man He had formed.". The story continues in Genesis 2:10 "And a river went out of Eden to water the garden; and from there it was parted and became into four heads." The part of the story that gives us a hint as to an approximate geographical location is Genesis 2:11 to 14, which read "The name of the first is Pison, and is composed of the whole land of Havilah, where there is gold. And the gold of that land is good, there is bdellium and onyx stone. And the name of the second river is Gihon, it is composed of the whole land of Ethiopia. and the name of the third river is Hiddekil, which go toward the east toward Assyria, and the fourth river is Euphrates." If we examine this passage carefully, and substitute the known geographical land marks we will find that the only river that compares to that in the scenario with respect to logistics and close proximity to the geographical names mentioned, is the Nile River. The Nile is the longest river on earth, and the only river in the world to flow from the south to the north. This northern flow fits the progression described in the story of the river of Eden. Starting from the origin of the Nile from Africa to the south the story is corroborated. There is certainly considerable amounts of gold in the southern region of Africa at the beginning of the Nile. Ethiopia was situated northward relative to the base of the Nile. Moving further northward up the Nile toward the east of it lies Assyria. Further north and east lies the Euphrates.

Ethiopia is mentioned in the Biblical text in the creation passage, and long before Egypt is ever referred to. A number of scholars, both ancient and modern, have come to the conclusion that the world's first civilization was created by the black people we call Ethiopian. It is certain that classical historians and geographers called the whole region from India to Egypt by the name Ethiopia, and in consequence they regarded the dark-skinned and black peoples who inhabited it as Ethiopians.

According to Herodotus and others, the Ethiopians inhabited Arabia, Egypt, India, Palestine, the Sudan, and Western Asia. In a publication in 1869 by John D. Baldwin, a member of the American Oriental Society, titled "Pre-Historic Nations", the author noted:

> "At the present time Arabia is inhabited by two [ethnic groups], namely the descendants of the old Adite, Kushite, or Ethiopian [group], known under various appellations, and dwelling chiefly at the south, east, and central parts of the country, but formerly supreme throughout the whole peninsula; and the Semitic Arabians of Mahomet's [group], found mainly in the Hejaz and at the north. Some districts are mixed, and since the rise of [Islam] the language known to us as Arabic, has wholly superseded the old Ethiopian or Kushite tongue.....To the Kushite [group] belongs the purest Arabian blood, and also that great and very ancient civilization whose

ruins abound in almost every district of the country"

Thousands of inscriptions have been collected in southwest Arabia, and they were found to resemble Ethiopic characters rather than what we know today as Arabic characters. These Ethiopic characters predate the so-called Arabic by one thousand years. It seems that in ancient times stretched across the warm belt of the globe form Africa to Malaya, were black skinned people who by the environmental and evolutionary processes, became transformed. It is believed that they gave rise to the so-called Hamitic stock of Africa, to the Dravidian peoples of India and to the intermediate dark people inhabiting the Arabian peninsula. Records also prove that there were two great migrations of lighter skinned people from the north. One of the migrations were the Mongoloids who transformed the dark belt beyond India, the other migration of Caucasoids created a wedge between India and Africa.

The fact the Biblical records show that Moses married the black skinned Zipporah, who was a Midianite from Arabia, demonstrates that at least during that time a very black skinned people could still be found in Arabia.

The ancient Egyptians were Africans, and their official language of communication, which expressed fundamental relationships and feelings, as well as beliefs was African in character. A very large number of the words in the language are monosyllabic, as opposed to the triliterality of the so-called Semitic family of languages, and were derived from the Predynastic Egyptians, who were Africans from the Great Lakes region. The monosyllabic words expressed fundamental African relationships, such as

Nu (Nau)	God matter/male
Nut (Nen)	God matter/female
khu	spirit
ba	soul
sba	stars
rae (Ra)	sun
pet	heaven
mu (nu)	water
ta	earth
khat	body
ab	heart
mut	mother
atef	father
sen	son
sent	daughter
hat	house
mer	love

The Nile River, travelling northward through Africa, unlike any other river in the world, is like a vast highway. In the past it served as a thruway for African peoples from western and eastern parts. Without doubt, the official written language of ancient Egypt was colored by the linguistical diversity of Africa as a whole, due to the mobility afforded them via the Nile River highway. A study of the African languages and dialects of the Nile Valley, and the language groups that migrated from it, will prove useful in understanding both the written and spoken language(s) of the ancient Egyptians.

There are also a number of triliteral root words in ancient Egyptian, perhaps demonstrating an ancient relationship with the so-called Semitic family of languages, as Hebrew, Aramaic, Amharic, Arabic etc., however, the predominance of the monosyllabic root words indicate a closer affinity with indigenous African languages of the southern regions of Africa.

LANGUAGE AND CULTURE

Literature is the inscribed language of a culture. The language of a people is a medium through which their culture, moral codes, and history, are preserved. From word usage, we can understand cultural concepts. Most of what we know about the ancient Egyptians, is revealed to us from ancient literature that they left behind. Other facts about the Egyptians we gather from what we know about the the culture of their modern day descendants, Africans.

We don't know when or how the human animal began speaking or writing, nor do we know when or how the many different languages developed. We know, however, that the Africans who comprised the Nile Valley civilization created a illustrative picture script called "hieroglyphics". They used symbols, images, natural objects, and animal figures (zootypes) that were indigenous to their African environment. Creatively, the picture script was used to convey human thoughts, and express human feelings. Ancient Egypt as part of the Nile Valley civilization, situated in Africa, was/is an integral part of African culture. Her language expressed the world in the image perceived by African people.

The wedge-shape marks called cuneiform, created by the Sumerians, is also a ancient form of writing. Scientist are not certain whether cuneiform predates the hieroglphics. This writer, however, based on the fact that the hieroglyps developed by Africans of the Nile Valley civilizations remains one of the most complex scripts ever designed, believe it to be older than cuneiform by virtue of that complexity, which can only be achieved over a long period of time. In addition, ancient records testify to the great wealth of African knowledge passed from earlier generations to other cultures, Sumeria included.

Stating that ancient Egypt was situated on the continent of Africa, does not totally clear up the language and cultural issues. Africa is inhabited by indigenous people, who speak almost a thousand different languages, and who have a wide range of cultural practices, as a consequence of antiquity.

Our contention is, Egypt was a society integrated with indigenous Africans from many parts of the continent, especially from the south. The Nile River is a natural thruway from the south portion of Africa to her most northern shores.
Other evidence, wall paintings and recovered statues, mummies, and art work, show the presence of several other African ethnic groups in Egypt. Such that the culture and

language was an amalgamation, of its conglomerated ethnicity. To take this point a step further, the development of the Egyptian picture writing known as hieroglyphics, we feel, was a measure to linguistically homogenize the delima of ethnic diversity, by creating a universal medium of communication with the creative aid of natural images and common objects to inscribe and record human speech, and convey human thoughts. It could take similar thoughts, words, and expressions, from different languages, and give them universal symbols, understood by all. Hieroglyphics is, therefore, more than just a form of writing, it is also a amalgamated language of communication that helped create one nation out of a linguistically diversified and ethnically pluralistic society, whose inhabitants filtered in via the Nile thruway. The advent of the hieroglyphics was a revolution in the recording of human speech, and the advancement of communication, which led to the development of the academia upon which human civilizations thrive.

The Egyptian hieroglyphics, are structured and have well defined grammatical form. Whole ideas can be expressed by the ideographs. The symbols could be used to represent figurative speech, or the picture scrip could represent sounds of human speech and then spell out words, as an alphabet system. Thus the versatile African picture script used four (4) modes of communication;

      1- plain imitation
      2- figurative speech
      3- coded messages, using certain rules
      4- sounds of human speech, alphabet system.

The animal images (zootypes) employed in the hieroglyphics writing was drawn directly from the types found in the African environment. There were several others used, some more or less common. Scientists of the day must have known quite a bit about the habits of the animals of the African continent, as demonstrated by the abstract concepts connected with the images when used in writing.

🦅	a	𝋃	b	⬜	h	⌒	k
◢	a	▢	p	𖤍	ḥ	△	ḳ
▬	ā	⌐	f	●	χ	⌒	t
\\	i	🦅	m	∫ and —	s	═ or)	t
\\\\	ī	∼∼	n	⊂⊃	Sh	⌒	d
🦉	u	⌒	r	⊥⊥⊥	Sh	⌐	z
𓃒	ū, ua (w)	🐟	l	△	q	🔪	j

A basic alphabet system composed of pictographs, the hieroglyphics used natural objects to record human sounds and spell words. Note the characteristic "Sh" sound and the pictograph from which it is derived. We find this letter in both Hebrew and Arabic almost unchanged, clearly demonstrating its derivation from the Egyptian hieroglyphics.

Apparently, the pictographs were designated alphabetic representation from the first letter of the word expressed by the pictograph, and or the first letter of the sound associated with the pictograph, e.g.,

PICTOGRAPH	EGYPTIAN NAME	ALPHABET
eagle (falcon)	Ahoom	A
owl	Mouloj	M
hand	Doode (Toote)	D (T)
water	Mu (Nu)	M (N)
potted plants	SHaesh	SH
viper	Fent	F
mouth	Ro (Lo)	R (L)

"A"

The **bird pictograph** represent the letter "A". However, the human mouth can express this particular sound in so many modified ways. It is believed to be an "A" sound which **borders on** a "O" sound, and is modified by dialect. The **reed (leaf)** is an "A" which **borders** on a "E" sound, and the **extended arm is long** "A" as in "April".

"T (D)"

"T" in the Egyptian word "toote" (**hand**) borders on a "D" sound and in translated words the "D" sound is sometimes expressed. The Egyptian name for **Pygmy** is "Tenk" or "Denk". This sound is best **expressed by the Spanish** "d", as in "dedo" (finger).

"R (L)"

The partially curled "R" is **interchangeable with** the "L", and thus the **mouth symbol** "Ro" is **also** "Lo". From the Egyptian word "lo" (mouth), joined with the Egyptian word "Go" or "Jo" (to speak, or voice) we derive the modern word "logo", "speech of mouth" or "word". Similarly, the word "Nile" is derived from the African Egyptian language. An Egyptian word for "river" is "eiro" or "eilo". Prefixed with the Egyptian "n", the word becomes "n-eilo", which literally means "the river, or our river". Thus, the modern word "Nile" is derived from "neilos", which was used by the Greeks. Many of the old Greek words used today are not Greek, but are in fact Egyptian words adopted by the Greeks

"SH"

This strong "SH", as in the Yoruba deities "SHango" and "O-SHun", is common to many African languages. Its special sound is represented by the pictograph of potted plants originating from the southern Nile. Both the Hebrew and Arabic letter "Shin" is directly derived from the hieroglyphic symbol of potted plants.

The advent of the hieroglyphic picture scrip by Africans created for the first time in known human history, a method to record human speech. It revolutionized communication between the the human specie. Its advent led to the further development of human culture, academia, and the radiation of civilization. The method was adopted by the world.

African people are extremely religious, and the picture scrip was extensively applied to expressing religious phenomena and philosophy. The word "hieroglyphics", we are told means sacred carving, from the Greek "hiero" (sacred) and "glyphe" (carving). The Greek word "hiero" may have been derived from the Egyptian root word "heru" or "helu" for "heaven or light". "Glyphe" bear some resemblance to the Egyptian "glep or grep" for "scroll or to roll up". Religious and thus sacred writings were written on scrolls that were rolled up and tied. A more accurate definition may be "heavenly scrolls", that were sacred by virtue of its heavenly connection. They were referred to as the "speech of the Divine or God" (metut nutr), or "the writing that brings life" (se-she nu per ankh).

When written on stone the hieroglyphics provided a permenant record. This permenant record is observed on monuments and temples throughout Egypt and the Nile valley, which stand today, thousands of years after they were erected. You might say that these were one of the first permenant historical documents known to the human kind. It is reasonable to believe that the early developers had written plans not only for the monuments, but for the inscriptions on them. Therefore, it is reasoned that the written plans didn't survive time as did the stone inscriptions, due to the fact that they were, perhaps, written on a more perishable type of material. We do know, when the hieroglyphics were not written on stone, it was written on paper made from the African papyrus plant, which of course will not survive as long as stone. Paper made from the papyrus was the first paper known to be introduced to human culture.

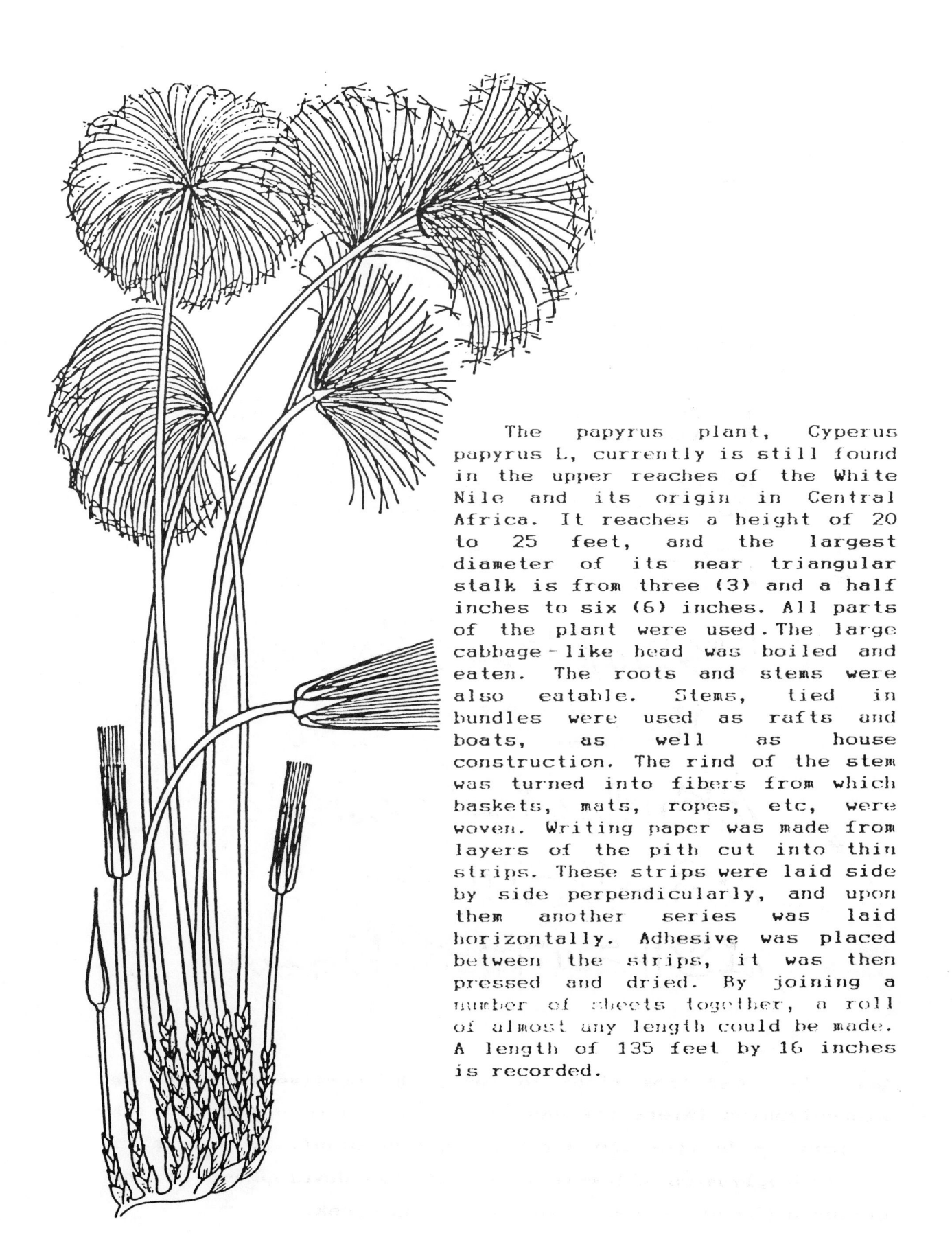

The papyrus plant, Cyperus papyrus L, currently is still found in the upper reaches of the White Nile and its origin in Central Africa. It reaches a height of 20 to 25 feet, and the largest diameter of its near triangular stalk is from three (3) and a half inches to six (6) inches. All parts of the plant were used. The large cabbage-like head was boiled and eaten. The roots and stems were also eatable. Stems, tied in bundles were used as rafts and boats, as well as house construction. The rind of the stem was turned into fibers from which baskets, mats, ropes, etc, were woven. Writing paper was made from layers of the pith cut into thin strips. These strips were laid side by side perpendicularly, and upon them another series was laid horizontally. Adhesive was placed between the strips, it was then pressed and dried. By joining a number of sheets together, a roll of almost any length could be made. A length of 135 feet by 16 inches is recorded.

Generally read from right to left, the cursive form of the hieroglyphics (hieratic) was transcribed with a pen and ink on paper made from the African papyrus plant. This form of the hieroglyphics ultimately led to the development of the common alphabet used both in Coptic and Greek.

Now if we transcribe these into hieroglyphics we obtain the following :—

1. a reed
2. a mouth
3. a hare
4. the wavy surface of water
5. see No. 4
6. a kind of vessel
7. an owl
8. a bolt of a door
9. a seated figure of a man
10. a stroke written to make the word symmetrical
11. see No. 1
12. a knee bone (?)
13. see No. 2.
14. a roll of papyrus tied up
15. an eye
16. see No. 6
17. a goose
18. see No. 9
19. see No. 4
20. a chair back
21. a sickle
22. an eagle
23. see No. 7
24. a tree
25. see No. 14
26. an axe
27. see No. 10.

The land of Egypt was called "Khem or Kham". Spelled in the hieroglyphics, the feminine article "t" was placed on the end to give us the word "Khem-t or Kham-t", as countries and land masses were denoted in the feminine gender. At the ending of the hieroglyphic word is the symbol of the circular enclosure of an African village, which denote a body of people or nation in the broader sense. The word "khem or kham" means black. The biblical name "Ham" from the Old Testament is derived from this Egyptian word. Scholars have argued over the use of this word by the ancients. They are certain that the word means black, however, some think that the Egyptians were referring to the blackness of the earth along the Nile. It is ludicrous to not see that the black skinned Egyptians were very much aware of their blackness, especially by comparison to lighter skinned neighbors. Clearly "Kham-t or Khem-t" is translated as the blackland. The simple fact that the Egyptians were a black skinned people, leaves us to believe that their designation of the term was a mere description of the inhabitants of the land. This word has found its way in modern usage in the word "chemistry". Chemistry as a science, was passed downed from the ancient Egyptians. Looking closely at the word and its phonetics, we find that "Khem" is the parent root of "Chem". We should not be surprised by this, for a class of Egyptian science was called "Al-kimmia" by the Arabs, which in translation means "the Black Arts". From this art "Alchemy" came into existence, followed by modern Chemistry.

Fragments of Egypt's West African Connection

It is almost impossible to find a single indigenous language in any region of Africa. This was true in the past and is also true today. African linguistics is a complicated matter. Scientist have not come up with an ideal grouping of African languages. Joseph Greenberg in 1963 suggested four major groups, Afro-Asiatic, Nilo-Saharan, Niger-Congo, and the Khoisan. The term "Afro-Asiatic" is an inappropriate terminology, and should be possibly changed to "Hamitic" and "Semitic". Modern science traces the origin of the human race from Africa and it stands to reason that human language can also be traced back to Africa. Therefore all African languages are related by virtue of the previous statement. Although the Egyptian language for the most part is classed as Hamitic, it also crosses the lines of other African language groups, Walaf for example. Walaf is a West Atlantic African language of the Niger-Congo group. Certainly we could find both close and distant relationships between other African languages and the official language of the Nile Valley Civilization. After all the Egyptians themselves were Africans, and their culture was African. this is why we find a similarity between the Yoruba culture with its system of orishas (deities) and the Egyptian culture. However, this writer is of the opinion that any attempts to find a single indigenous African language as a prototype of the ancient Egyptian will fail. The reason being, as stated earlier, the Egyptian language is a conglomeration of several African languages with strong overtones of the dominant African group of the region or era.

Classed in the Kwa sub-group of the Niger-Congo language group, the Yorubas cultural connection with the Egyptians is evident from their folk stories. The Yorubas have several stories about their history, one of them described in Samuel Johnson's "History of the Yorubas" tells that the Yorubas sprang from Lamurudu (Namurudu, a dialectic modification of the name Nimrod). Lamurudu or Namurudu was one of the kings of Mecca whose offspring were: Oduduwa, the ancestors of the Yorubas, the Kings of Gogobiri and the Kukawa (two ethnic groups in the Hausa country). The two Hausa groups still today have the same facial marks, despite their distance from each other and the lapse of time. At what period Lamurudu reigned is uncertain. The crowned prince Oduduwa held fast to the ancient Traditional religion. He was very influential and had many followers. He attempted to transform the state religion to the traditional form. Oduduwa's priest, Asara (Osar, Osirus) had a son Braima who was brought up into the new religion of Islam. He destroyed many idols and was sentenced to die by fire. The two groups had large followers and this action brought on a civil war between the Traditionalist led by Lamurudu and the Moslem groups. Lamurudu was killed and all his children and sympathizers were expelled from the town. Oduduwa and his children went to Ile Ife.

According to the story of of Oduduwa the Hausas are connected to the Yorubas. Today the Hausas are West African muslims and their language is written in a specie of Arabic, which is not readily understood by those familiar with only the modern Arabic script. The kingdom of South Central Sudan (south of Egypt) later comprised the Hausa Bakwai, was seven (7) historical Hausa states. Such that the Hausa are clearly connected to the East. That the Yorubas were also associated with the East is consistent with the story, and is indicated by their habits, manners and customs. Studies suggest that they came from Nubia or Upper Egypt. It is very possible that they were found in and around Mecca. There seems to be a connection to the family line of the Egyptian conqueror Nimrod. According to Egyptian records, Nimrod was associated with west African people.

In the XXI Egyptian Dynasty, a west African people called Tehenu, were warriors in the Egyptian armed forces, and their military leader was called "Me" (Meshwesh). From these people came another dynamic leader named Buyuwawa, who formed a princely line. The Harpason Stela in the Louvre gives the line of descent from Buyuwawa through several generations. His descendant in the 4th generation, a prince called Shashank, married an Egyptian princess, became the "Great Chief of Me", and transmitted his title to his son Nimrod. Nimrod in turn transmitted his title to his son, Shashank II. Shashank II founded the XXII Egyptian Dynasty. The Tehenu people were related to the Egyptians as proven by the fact that they used Egyptian names, and practiced Egyptian culture. The story of Lamurudu or Namurudu seem to suggest a relationship between the rulers of the XXII Dynasty and the Yoruba people from West Africa. Apparently, prior to that time the Yoruba were in both Egypt and West Africa and at a certain period there was a great migration of the Yoruba from the east to west Africa.

Early writing of the Nile Valley Civilization was a collection of instructions, codes for human behavior, religious philosophy, and scientific materials. They recorded information on mathematics, astronomy, medicine, physics, and architecture. Accurate systems of measurements, efficient devices for the transport of building materials were developed. It is a wonder how they were able to cut solid stone into appropriate forms and sizes and then set these heavy stones into position. They developed the use of addition, subtraction, multiplication, and the use of fractions, which enabled them to calculate the areas of triangles, squares, rectangles and circles. The value of "π" in modern circular mathematics was determined by the early Africans of the Nile Valley. Astronomers charted the heavens and identified the fixed stars, and devised instruments to calculate the positions of fixed stars and planets that were not visible. The pyramids were so designed that its base is a square whose perimeter is equal to the circumference of a circle inscribed within that square, and whose radius is the pyramids height. This is known as the squaring of a circle. From a Egyptian medical papyrus thousands of years old, acquired by the the American Egyptological Society, over 48 cases of injuries were systematically recorded. Included were methods for adjusting broken bones, reducing fractures with splints and casts, bringing open wounds together with sutures and clamps or a kind of adhesive plaster. Many other ancient text books were uncovered, giving remedies for all types of gynecological problems to the growth of hair. Without the art of writing the ancient Africans would have never reached such a high state of development.

The Chester Beattty Papyrus edited by A.H Gardiner (IV, No. 3) makes reference to older literary works by African writers as Zedefra, Imhotep, Nefri, Akhte, Ptah-hotep, Ptah-huti and others, whose works are apparently lost. We can consider these men as the first professional writers ever mentioned in history. Other works have been passed down to us in manuscript form written on papyrus. Such works must have been part of the temple libraries or libraries of the nobility. It is an established fact that literary works were to be found in schools where students learned and copied them, and therefore, in those cases where only one manuscript was found we must suppose that other copies were either lost or destroyed. These ancient literary works were read and enjoyed by people in the most ancient times, and long before the Bible stories were put into writing

The hieroglyphic literature was written in short and often independent sentences. Both simple and abstract ideas could easily be expressed. The writer could express himself or herself vividly and lyrically. Pictures with captions were used for the first time. Today, this convention is still employed by every publication in the world. Sample excerpt from texts readily demonstrates sentence structure, moral concepts, special codes of conduct about dealing with the elderly, matters pertaining to marital situations, and even historical notes.

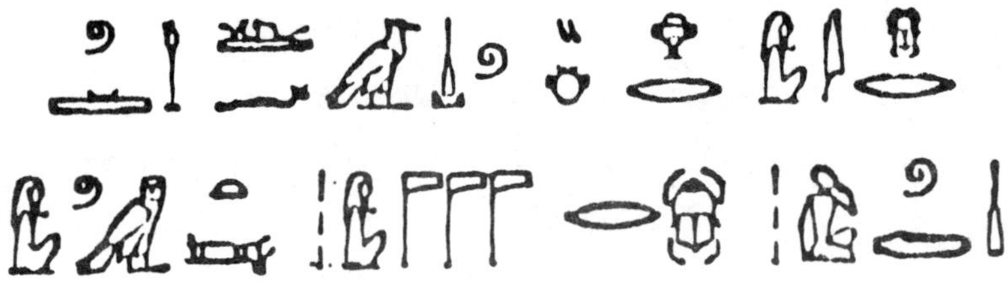

Read from the right to the left

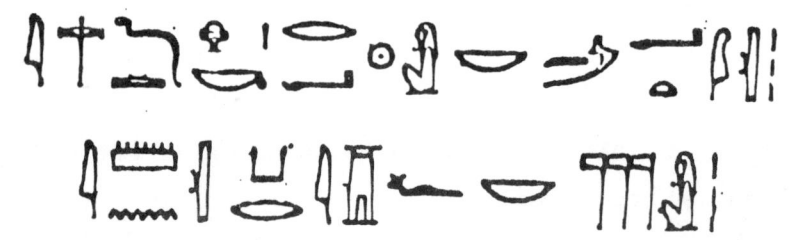

Read from the left to the right

Read from top right to left    Read from top left to right

Today, we would go to a library to view creative art and visit a museum for fine art. An ancient Egyptian interested in language and the arts need only to walk into the temples. There, surrounded by immaculate structures of art and picturesque hieroglyphics, ones entire being becomes consumed by the ubiquity of it all. Students would feel as though they were in a house of learning, as the structures themselves revealed lectures on several topics. On the tomb of Seti I, of the 19th Dynasty we are given an introduction to human genesis as interpreted through the religious dogma of the times. The picturesque temple graphically display royal representatives of four (4) ethnic groupings, who are, from right to left; the Timihu, Nehesiu, Amu, and the Remtu.

The man choosen by Hatshepsut to lead the Punt Expedition was from a royal group of people in Egypt. In the "Book of Pylons", a hieroglyphic inscription tells an allegorical story of the creation of four (4) ethnic groups, the "Rethu", "Aamu", "Nehhesiu", and the "Themihu". Drawings of each ethnic group were found on the walls of the tomb of Seti. The Rethu looked very much like the Africans of Somali or the Central Sudan, and the Danakil of modern Ethiopia. The hairy, flat aqualine nosed group were the Aamu. Wearing ostrage feathers, a long robe styled with one sleeve, tattoos on their bodies, were the light skinned Themihu. With a white linen skirted apparel hanging ankle length, a beautifully colored bandana draped over the shoulder, matching a waist belt and strap that hung just past the knees, the jet black Nehhesiu (Nahhasiu) group were noble in appearance, and represented a broad cross section of the Africans of the southern Nile.

This creation story sets up a scenario in which the "soul of the divine spirit", "Horu" or "Oru", proclaim; the Rethu were created by the "tears" or "light rays" from the eye of Horu; the Aamu and the light complexion Themihu were created by the union of Horu and the feminine deity "Sekhet", who personified the burning and sometimes destructive power of the sun. But of the Nehhesiu, Horu says in the hieroglyphic passage;

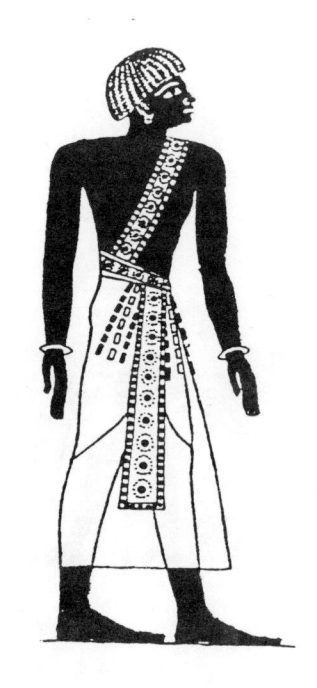

Nehesu

nt then
of ye (you);

    nenhu-nekht na   er-then   hotep-a m hrah
I empowered primordial   to make ye,   I was pleased of
    matter   the millions

  pert   am-a   m   ren-ten   n   Nehhesiu
that came   from me   in your name of Nehhesiu
forth

"Nehhesiu" as spelled in the hieroglyphics is derived from the word "hehessi" or "hehessiu", "of favor", "favored ones", or "chosen ones". The alphabetical symbol of the bird in the word is "Neh-" or "Nah-". Joined to "hesiu", we arrive at the name "Nehhesiu" (Nahhasiu). Words such as "nehesiu", "nahasiu", "nahashi" or "neheshi", mean chosen, to be of favor, and strong. It is clear that blacks were considered to be the chosen people, or at lease by the Africans who formulated the creation story in the Book of Pylons. Historically, ethnic groups in a position of power perceived themselves as superior in every way, to those dominated by them. So it was, by the early African of the Nile Valley Civilization, and so it is, today, by the white ruling ethnic groups.

1. an shenena noutre

2. an nekbah-a hemt thabah

3. an semamtem-a nerti sep

4. an tha-au-a

5. an as-stha-ab-a

6. an ari-a asefetwr

(1)-I have not cursed God.
(2)-I have not defiled the wife of another man
(3)-I have not commited murder
(4)-I have not robbed
(5)-I have not judged hastily
(6)-I have not done evil

1. am   an-k   hemeswr   au   nia   hae   au-f

2. aaetu   arek   em   re   pu   au-f

3. saeuia-k   aer-f   em   aaetu

4. tuf   ukha-a-kh-nek   gera

(1)-Thou should not sit while being the younger, while another standing, he being
(2)-older than thou, even if it be of he
(3)-that thou are greater than he in position
(4)-to him. Thou should follow him in silence.

1. ar aaea-k   mekhet   nezesuwr-k

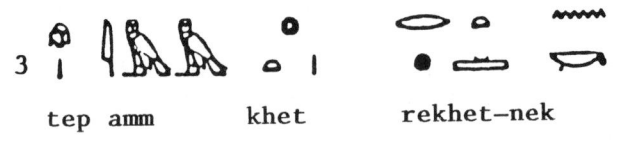

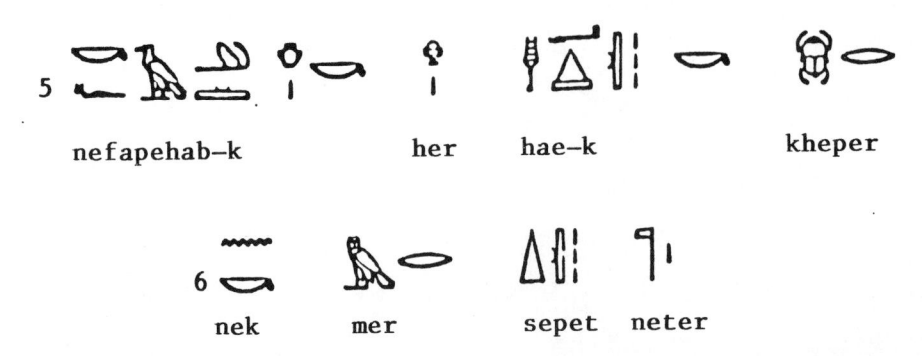

2. ari-k   khet   mekhet   geaetwr

3. tep amm   khet   rekhet-nek

4. em seshau   kheperit-nek   khennetum

5. nefapehab-k   her   hae-k   kheper

6. nek   mer   sepet   neter

(1)- If thou hast become great after thou was of little means
(2)- and made wealth after poverty
(3)- lead in the city and take heed that thou
(4)- do not turn to profit, having become dominant, let not
(5)- be hardened thy heart through thy elevation
(6)- for thou has become only a stewart of the goods of God.

1	khat	ar	aqer-k	ger-k	het-k	mer-a
2	-k	hemt-k	m	khenp shet	khat-s	hebes sa-s
3	pekhret-uten	pu	nt	ha-s	merhet-ab-s	
4	auuabs	ter-renpt	n	ounnet-k	ahet pu	khut
5	n	neba-s	amm	an -k	n	hae serit

(1)-If thou are to be prosperous in thy house love
(2)-thy wife without insincerity, fill her belly, cloth her back (body).
(3)-bestow upon her, beautiful scented oils for the flesh of her limbs.
(4)-Make her happy in her heart, during the time of thy existence on earth, for she will magnify the estate
(5)-of her lord, be not harsh, but gentleness will----

1. seher se re sekhem atheta-s
2. zaethau-s pu arit-s maariaa-s souahuah-s
3. pu em het-k shennaei-s nu pu khat
4. ser en aeui-s shen-nnet-s ari nes meri

(1) ----send her on her path, violence will push her away.
(2) -as a powerful wind. Sustain her with that which she eye with her eyes.
(3) -In thy house, call upon her affectionately, caress her breast
(4) -and touch her hands in embrace, speak softly to her, make love to her.

1. nuk pu khper

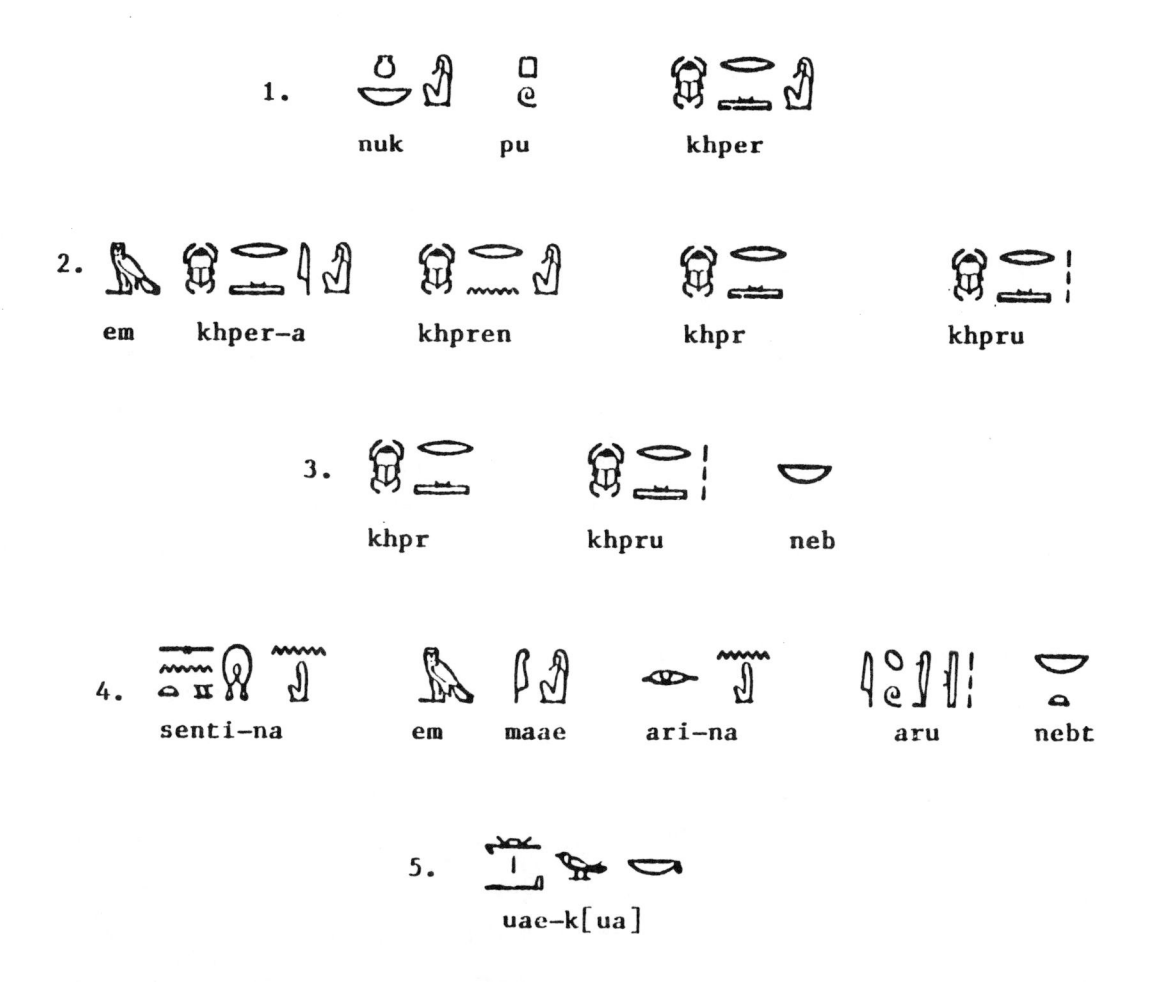

2. em khper-a khpren khpr khpru

3. khpr khpru neb

4. senti-na em maae ari-na aru nebt

5. uae-k[ua]

1- I am He who came into Being
2- In the form of Being, I became the creator of Being
3- The creator of Being all (all being)
4- I laid the foundation in Righteousness I fashioned forms all (all forms)
5- I was alone.

This passage expresses ancient Egyptian monotheism.

Pigmy Dance of God

The "Pigmy Dance Of God", was a special religious dance done by the Pigmies of Africa. Ancient records clearly show that the Egyptian kings saught after the Pigmies from the land of the spirits to perform a sacred dance before their court. Singing and dancing were and are today an important part of the culture of African people. Not unlike other African people, the Egyptians required dancing at their festivities, weddings and funerals. Inscriptions from the tomb of Heru-khuf at Aswan tells that the govenor of Elephantine was ordered to bring a Pigmy before Pepi II, the fifth king of the 6th Dynasty, to dance at a ceremony. The records cite that Assa, the eighth king of the 5th Dynasty greatly rewarded his minister Ba-ur-Tettet for bringing the Pigmy before him. Pepi II informs his minister that greater honors would be conferred upon him should he succeed in presenting a Pigmy before the king, and in good health. It is quite apparent that the Pigmy was very important to a special religious rite, and the king saw it as an honor to have the "Pigmy Dance of God" performed at his court. It is written "He who is between the thighs of Nut is the Pigmy who dance like God and who pleases the heart of the gods before his great throne."

(1)-It is the desire of the Majesty to see in the flesh, this Pigmy as an (2)-offering from the Bata and Punt lands. If you arrive at (3)-your country and from the palace you bring this Pigmy (4)-with you alive and in good health, the Majesty (5)- will make you greater than was made the treasurer (6)-Ba- ur- Tattu in the time of Assa when he pleased the heart (7)- of his (Majesty) upon seeing this Pigmy.

NTR

A common word given by the ancient Egyptians to the Supreme Power, gods or orishas, spirits of every kind, beings of all sorts and forms, which possessed superhuman powers, was "nuter" or "neter" (syllables ntr). Neter was represented by the hieroglyphic symbol of an axe. As a primordial symbol of power and authority, the axe, symbolized the operative powers of all things, that energized the Creation, and is the Divine Force perpetuating re-generation and change. It is the power, strength, and will, derived from the Supreme Power, making all that it empowers, divine. The Divine Power, neter, is kept in being and wholeness by maintaining its correlation with the Supreme Existence, from which it is derived. The word, neter, as a whole concept, can be understood through the religious and philosophical perceptions of the African mind, which balances the world of spirits and Supreme Being. Nutr (Neter) for the most part is untranslatable in the English language.

Despite the belief in spirit forces as gods or orishas, the ancient Egyptian religion was basically monotheistic. Notwithstanding the elaborate system of symbols and ceremonies, Egyptian monotheism always maintained its place in the mind of those who were sufficiently educated to understand the ideas which the symbols represented. Educated Egyptians never confounded their gods or orishas with their Supreme Being.

The Living Word

Writing brought human words to life. Developing an ingenious system to record human speech was like a child's first step, in that it was merely a prelude to more magnificent things to come. Symbols and images previously confined to the individual human mind, could as a result of the evolution of writing, be collectively shared with others. It offered a new medium in which ideas could be expressed, transferred, and preserved verbatim with more precision than oral traditional means. Through this new medium the secrecy of the sacred could be maintained by the symbols inherent in the writing system. The ancients took the opportunity to record the drama acted out in the heavens, with the motion of the celestial bodies, and the passing of day into night. Human history and development were inscribed on natural objects and material to serve future generations to come. Writing led to the production of books which in turn gave birth to reading and literature. Early literature expressed religious dogma coupled with ethical codes of conduct. Scientific data was intimately connected with religious philosophy. Modern classical subjects as biology, chemistry, physics and mathematics were integral parts of sacred religious institutions, which were known as the Mystery Schools. These schools or universities maintained great libraries with books on many subjects. All of the pre-Christian writers were trained either directly or indirectly through the Mystery Schools. Everything concerning the Mystery Schools were under strict secrecy. There were many truths contained in their writings which were inconvenient for the authorities to generally know, and there were other things although false (in form) were best for the people to believe. Christian literature maintained this convention of secrecy as exhibited in the book of Matthew chapter 13 verses

9 to 11, in which the disciples of Jesus inquire as to the reason that the people are spoken to in parables, to which Jesus replies in chapter 11; "Because it is given unto you to know the mysteries of the kingdom of heaven but to them it is not given." The connection of the Mystery Schools and Christianity were summed up by Saint Augustine who wrote; "What is now called the Christian Religion has existed among the ancients and was not absent from the beginning of the human race until Christ came in the flesh, from which time the religion which already existed, began to be called Christian." Through writing, words came to life in books that were passed on through the ages. From Africa came the first written word, and through the Coptic language, which is the final stage of the hieroglyphics, early Christian literature was memorialized.

Lotus and papyrus flowers. Painted tomb ceiling. Thebes. XVIIIth Dynasty.

Coptic Language

Coptic, a modern descendant from the ancient Egyptian language, is a classical African language, inriched with the early history of Africa, and her historical experiences with other peoples of the world. It is a language cloaked in the African personality, yet not so rigid as not to be open to other languages. Dynamic, as most languages are, Coptic not only absorbed words from other languages, it imparted words of its own to languages such as Hebrew, Aramaic, Arabic, Persian, Greek, as well as other indigenous African languages. Modern day Copts claim descent from the ancient Egyptians. Through miscegenation, modern Copts in Egypt appear much lighter in complexion than their black ancestors. The term Coptic is a word that has become synonymous with both Egyptian, and Christian. The name and its history will prove extremely interesting, and historically significant, as far as ancient Egypt and the spread of Christianity is concerned.

As a language, Coptic is extinct, and is only used in the liturgy of the Coptic Church. It is a modern descendant of the ancient Egyptian language, expressed in the hieroglyphics. Currently, several dialects of Coptic have been identified, and they are:

1- **Fayyumic**, survived on the West Bank until the 8th century
2- **Asyutic**, (sub-Akhmimic), spoken in Asyut, in and around Akhmim (Upper Egypt), flourished in the 4th century. Contains works as:

      a- Gospel of John
      b- Acts of the Apostle
      c- some Gnostic documents

3- **Akhmimic**, spoken in Akhmim
4- **Bashmuric**, western delta, and Alexandria
5- **Bohairic**
6- **Memphitic**, Memphis
7- **Sahidic** (Thebaic), Thebes

The Coptic language evolved from the official language of the African civilization of Egypt. Its script evolved from the parent pictographic hieroglyphics. Its flexibility allowed it to absorb expressions and words from other languages and cultures. During the Egyptian period, Africa was still the center of academia and culture. People came from all parts of the world to learn from her wealth of knowledge and wisdom. The Greeks were no exception to this, they too went to school in Africa. It has often been said, by modern western scholars that the Coptic alphabet was derived from the Greek alphabet. However, statements from the ancient Greek writer Herodotus contridict this notion. The contribution of the Greek culture to Christianity, philosophy, and world civilization has been grossly over rated. This was done in part to satisfy a western need to have a western role model rather than an African one.

Ancient Greek historians consistently credited the Africans from Egypt for development of science, philosophy, religion, and civilization. One cannot conceive of the development of civilization without writing. It is a well known fact that the Africans from the Nile valley developed the art of writing. In fact they had several writing systems derived from the hieroglyphics. Herodotus and Diodorus Siculus, two ancient Greek writers attribute an Egyptian from the African city of Thebes named Cadmus, with bringing letters to the Greeks and forming a colony in Greece. He established the Greek city of Thebes. These same Greek writers state that prior to Cadmus coming to Greece, writing did not exist there. Cadmus is also referred to in Greek mythology as having brought letters to the Greeks. It stands to reason that the Greeks obtained their method of recording human speech from the Egyptians, as confirmed by Greek writers themselves. Thus the Coptic alphabet is not derived from the Greek alphabet as is always expressed by western scholars, rather the reverse appears to be the case. We know that the ancient Egyptians used several writing systems, which were derived from the hieroglyphics. An examination of the hieratic, the cursive form of the hieroglyphics, shows that the Coptic script was derived from it, or at least in part. Ultimately the modern alphabet used throughout the western world evolved from the Coptic script.

The very first letter of the Coptic alphabet, "A" is derived from the pictographic bird in the hieroglyphics. This zootype represented the sound of the letter "A" in the ancient Egyptian language. Its lower case "a" corresponds to the symbol of a man seated, and represent the Coptic personal pronoun suffix "a". One only need to look at the hieratic symbol of the seated man to be satisfied that this is in fact the case. The Coptic letter "P" (R) is clearly derived from the hieratic "mouth" symbol. With further study, examples demonstrating the derivation of the Coptic from the hieroglyphics or the hieratic can be found for each and every Coptic letter.

Coptic has a alphabet consisting of thirty one letters

as opposed to twenty four letters of the Greek alphabet. Seven of the Coptic letters were not used in Greek.

ϣ ϥ ϩ ϫ ϭ ϯ

Seven other letters were used as vowels.

Α Ε Η Ι Ο Υ Ω

Coptic Dialects

The dialects differ in phonetics and vocabulary but are basically the same as far as grammatical arrangement of words, and all are believed to have derived from what is called late Egyptian or the standard language of the 19th and 20th dynasties (about 1400 to 1200 B.C.). Coptic is a rich language that has had contact with every dominant ancient language group, and as a result has influenced many languages, as well as being influenced by them. It is a classical African language and has retained the monosyllabic root words derived from her African ancestors to the south near the great African lakes at the base of the Nile River.

In that many Coptic scholars of old were also well versed in Greek as well, it should not be surprising to find several Greek words and terminology expressed in Coptic, just as one would find words and terms in every language in the world that were taken from other language groups to which it was in contact with. Likewise, the Greek language has borrowed an enormous amount of Coptic words, several that have been Greek-ized and mistaken for pure Greek words. The fact that ancient Greeks had an early contact with African colonizers, the Greek city of Thebes for example, lent itself to the incorporation of African words into the Greek language. Thus by the time that Alexander the Great's armies entered Egypt, the Greek language had already borrowed a number of African words. Also, prior to this time there were a number of Greeks in African schools. It would stand to reason that they had to study the Egyptian language. For those Greeks who settled in Africa prior to Alexander, naturally their already mixed Greek would be further altered by the absorption of words from the dominant culture of Egypt. Western scholars tend to maximize the influence of the Greek on the Coptic and minimize the reverse, and in so doing credit the Greeks with words found common to both languages. This is not to deny that both languages borrowed from each other, as such is the dynamics of all languages, but logic suggest that the least gains more from the greater than the reverse. In this case the Coptic has a more extensive written and archaeological history than the Greek language. For a time both languages existed side by side, as a result of the Greeks coming to the forefront of power. Oftentimes one found books written in both Coptic and Greek. Many times only a Coptic version was found. Western scholars speculate that the Greek version was lost, and that the Coptic version was copied from this Greek version never proven to have existed in the first place. Again common logic suggest that much of the material previously attributed to the Greeks, were more than likely copied from the Coptic. Simply because words contained in a particular Coptic manuscript appear to be derived from the Greek does not indicate that the manuscript was originally composed in Greek.

Coptic and Hieroglyphics

The nouns of the language have distinct forms for plural, but many can be used as singular or plural. The distinct plurals, however show a bewildering variety of formations. Definite articles singular and plural are distinctive, and differentiate gender. There are few adjectives, but this can also be expressed with the Coptic preposition. Conjugation of verbs are elaborate, which are prefixed to express person, number, gender, tense, and mood. Adverbs, prepositions, and conjunctions are used extensively. Prepositions have distinct forms for nouns and pronoun objects. A common denominator of many African languages is that they are agglutinative, their syntax being affected entirely by prefixes and suffixes, and Coptic is no exception to this rule. Coptic has retained most if not all of its hieroglyphics grammatical forms. The distinctive grammatical articles, singular and plural, definite and indefinite are exactly the same in Coptic and the hieroglyphics. Prefixes, suffixes, verbs, adverbs, conjunction, nouns, pronouns, etc., have been remarkably preserved from the hieroglyphics to the Coptic. One only need to compare the hieroglyphics personal pronouns, verb suffixes and prefixes, and auxiliary verbs to convince oneself how almost unchanged is the grammar of the Coptic language from its hieroglyphics form.

Forming new words to express newer ideas was easily incorporated into the Coptic language. The very agglutinative nature of the language allowed for the formation of a variety of expressions.

Herui   Qebti
                          (Coptos)

The name Coptic (Koptik)

The name Coptic (Koptik) is derived from the city of Coptos which was the capitol of the fifth nome (providence, or city-state), Horu-i. which was situated in Upper or southern Egypt. The 4th nome of southern Egypt, called "Uas" and its capitol Thebes, and the 5th nome "Horu-i" whose capitol was Coptos, together were powerful administrative and and religious centers. These centers were often considered together. Perhaps this explains why together they were called "Kham-ur" (Budge. Gods of the Egyptians I). Kham is an old indigenous African name for Egypt. The "-ur" on the end denote, "ancient or great". Thus the 4th and 5th nomes of Upper Egypt were called "ancient Egypt" (Kham-ur). The Hebrew word "Ham" appears to have derived from the Egyptian word Kham, both referring to "black".

      Qbt   Gbt   Gbti

    The hieroglyphic consonants which spell the name "Coptos", are equivalent to "Qbtit, Kbtit, Gbtit". Coptos, is cited in reference as Koptitac, as well as Koptus (Kobtus), Kubt (Qubt), Kubti, Qubti, Gubti, and Copts. The reasons for the various spellings, are the phonetic similarity between the sounds of "k", "q", and "c", as "king", "queen", and "came". Through phonetic decay or perhaps due to its pronunciation, "g" as in "get" was sometimes interchanged with "k", "q", and "c" sounds. There is also a phonetic similarity between the "b" and "p" sounds, as "b" in "boat, bat, bet", and "p" in "poke, pat, pet". "Qu-b-ti" and "Qu-p-ti" sounds almost identical, such that "b" and "p" sounds were also interchanged. Hense, the following phonetically are one and the same;

                Q-b-tit Q-p-tit
                K-b-tit K-p-tit
                G-b-tit G-p-tit
                Ku-b-t   Ku-p-t
                Qu-b-t   Qu-p-t
                Gu-b-t   Gu-p-t

From these are derived the modern English word "Copt" or "Coptic, otherwise spelled "Kopt" or "Koptik".

Coptic and Egypt

The origin of words can be demonstrated by analysing its elements, by pointing out the root or primitive on which it is based, or by referring to a earlier form in its parent language. We contend, that our modern word "Egypt" is descended from the ancient Egyptian language, and from the same root that the word "Coptos" was derived. Kubti, Qubti, and Gubti, as root to the word "Copti", and thus, Coptic, is also the root of the word "Egypt". This becomes apparent when we break down the old Greek word for Egypt;

Αιγυπτιος

We must always bear in mind that the Greek language was influenced by the Egyptian language since the time that the alphabet was introduced in Greece by African colonizers. It would stand to reason that the terms used by the Greeks to represent the Egyptians would come from the Egyptian language itself. It is logical to assume that outsiders would identify a people by their administrative center. Gupti or Qubti was in fact an administrative center during the time of the Greeks. Separating the Greek prefix "Ai-" and the suffix "-os" returns us to the African root of the word.

Ai- gupti -os

Our root is derived from the name of an ancient religious center visited by the Greeks, and where many went for schooling. It was only natural for the Greeks to refer to the Egyptians by their administrative and religious center. In our modern transcription of the word, the Latin "y" was substituted for the vowel "u" in the root "gupti", to give "gypti" or "gypt". This simple phonetic substitution, merely adjusted the vowel sound to the Latin script. Thus from "Aiguptios" (Αιγυπτιος) came our modern word "Egypt".

Arab literature refer to the Egyptians as "Kobts" or "Qobts", translated as "Copts" in English. These Copts were Christian Egyptians, and the word became synonymous with Egyptian.

```
Egyptian   Greek Root   Arab
Qubti >    <gupti       < Qubt
Kubti >                 < Kubt

Ai-gupti-os -------> Egypt, in Greek
Qubt        -------> Copt, in Arabic
```

Therefore, the African root word "Qubti or Kubti", the name of the capital of the 5th nome of southern Egypt, which was part of a great administrative center called "Kham-ur", is the precursor of both the words Egypt and Coptic. Therefore both words are one and the same, and even to this day Coptic is Egyptian and vise versa. Further, Shenouda III the current Pope of the Alexandria Coptic Church stated in 1977 at a lecture at the University of Michigan, that Copt and Egypt are one word (see Divine Liturgy of St. Basil the Great, St. Mark Orthodox Coptic Church, Troy Michigan).

Coptic Monosyllabic Root Verbs

The Coptic retained its large number of basic monosyllabic words as found in the hieroglyphics, and other indigenous African languages.

COPTIC		TRANSLATION
ⲁⲓ	ai	to do
ⲁⲛϩ	anh	to live
ⲉⲣ	er	to be, make
ⲉⲛ	en	to lead
ϥⲓ	fi	to bear
ⲕⲓⲙ	kim	to move
ⲕⲟⲧ	kot	to turn
ⲗⲱⲕ	look	to be soft, fresh
ⲙⲟⲩ	mou	to die
ⲛⲁⲩ	nau	to see
ⲟⲗ	ol	to hear
ⲟⲩⲱ	ouoo	to cease, stay
ⲡⲱϩ	pooh	to break, burst
ⲥⲙⲟⲩ	smou	to bless
ⲧⲱⲕ	took	to be strong, thick
ϣⲉ	she	to go
ϣⲓ	shi	to measure
ϯ	di, ti	to give
ⲥⲉ	se	to drink
ϫⲉⲙ	djem, jem	to find
ϫⲏ	khae	to create, establish
ϫⲓ	dji, ji	to give
ϩⲓ	hi	to fall, to cast
ϧⲁ	kha	to leave

Many monosyllabic words in the Coptic express common ancient words, derived from its African parent language further to the south east.

ⲣⲏ, (rae) the sun
ⲫⲉ, (phe) the heaven
ϫⲱ, (jo) the head
ϭⲣⲉ, (khre) food
ϩⲣⲉ, (hre)   "
ⲙⲱⲟⲩ, (moou) water
ϩⲏⲧ, (haet) heart

Through agglutination, Coptic words are formed.

ⲙⲱⲟⲩ-ϩⲱⲟⲩ = rain
mou - hou
water - moisture

ⲟⲩⲱⲙ-ⲛϩⲏⲧ = repent
ouom - nhaet
consume - the heart

ⲙⲁⲛ-ϭⲓ-ⲥⲙⲏ, = a place of hearing
man - gi - smae (a hearing)
a place - to give - voice

ⲙⲁⲛ-ϯ-ϩⲁⲡ, = a tribunal
man - ti - hap
a place - to give - judgment

ⲉⲣ-ⲙⲉⲑⲣⲉ, = to testify
er - methre
to be - witness

ϯ-ⲱⲟⲩ, = to give glory
ti - oou
   to give - glory

ϯ-ⲧⲟⲧ, = to help
ti - tot
  to give - hand

ϫⲉⲙ-ⲛⲟⲙϯ, = to comfort
jem - nomti
to find - consolation

ϭⲛⲉ-ϫⲱ, = subject
gne - jo
   to bow - head

ϭⲓ-ⲥⲙⲏ, = to hear
gi - smae
to receive - voice

ⲉⲣ-ⲟⲩⲱⲓⲛⲓ, = to enlighten
er - ouoini
  to make - light

ϩⲓ-ⲱⲛⲓ, = to stone
hi - oni
 to cast - stone

57

Agglutinative formation of words in the African language of the Egyptians readily lent itself to the development of various classes of words, very much like Ki-Swahili which also has word classes

Some words are formed by placing ⲙⲁ (a place) along with ⲛ before it.

ⲙⲟⲛⲓ, to feed	ⲙⲁⲛ-ⲙⲟⲛⲓ, pasture, a place to feed
moni	man-moni
ⲉⲛⲕⲟⲧ, sleep	ⲙⲁⲛ-ⲉⲛⲕⲟⲧ, bed, place to sleep
snkot	man-sncot
ⲥⲱⲛⲉ, bound	ⲙⲁⲛ-ⲥⲱⲛⲉ, prison, place of binding
soonh	man-soonh
ⲫⲱⲧ, a flight	ⲙⲁⲛ-ⲫⲱⲧ, refuge, a place to flee to
phoot	man-phoot
ϣⲱⲡⲓ, to inhabit	ⲙⲁⲛ-ϣⲱⲡⲓ, a habitation, tabernacle
shoopi	man-shoopi

When words are compounded with ⲙⲁⲓ (a lover of), we obtain the following:

ⲧⲁⲓⲟ, honor	ⲙⲁⲓ-ⲧⲁⲓⲟ, a lover of honor
taio	mai-taio
ϩⲁⲧ, silver	ⲙⲁⲓ-ϩⲁⲧ, greed, a lover of silver
hat	mai-hat
ϣⲉⲙⲙⲟ, a stranger	ⲙⲁⲓ-ϣⲉⲙⲙⲟ, hospitable
shemmo	mai-shemmo

The negative ⲁⲧ prefixed render the following:

ⲕⲓⲙ, to move	ⲁⲧ-ⲕⲓⲙ, immovable
kim	at-kim
ⲙⲟⲩ, to die	ⲁⲧ-ⲙⲟⲩ, immortal
mou	at-mou
ⲛⲁⲩ, to see	ⲁⲧ-ⲛⲁⲩ, invisible
nau	at-nau
ⲡⲉⲧϩⲱⲟⲩ, evil	ⲁⲧ-ⲡⲉⲧϩⲱⲟⲩ, innocent
pethoou	at-pethoou
ⲥⲁϫⲓ, a word	ⲁⲧ-ⲥⲁϫⲓ, mute
saji	at-saji

The prefix ⲙⲉⲧ or ⲙⲉⲑ gives:

ⲙⲉⲑⲣⲉ, witness	ⲙⲉⲧ-ⲙⲉⲑⲣⲉ, testimony
methre	met-methre
ⲙⲁⲧⲟⲓ, soldier	ⲙⲉⲧ-ⲙⲁⲧⲟⲓ, an army
matoi	met-matoi
ⲟⲩⲁⲓ, one	ⲙⲉⲧ-ⲟⲩⲁⲓ, unity
ouai	met-ouai
ⲟⲩⲣⲟ, king	ⲙⲉⲧ-ⲟⲩⲣⲟ, kingdom
ouro	met-ouro
ⲣⲉⲙϩⲉ, free	ⲙⲉⲧ-ⲣⲉⲙϩⲉ, freedom
remhe	met-remhe

To express that one is a native of a country, or belong to a specific human category, the prefix ⲣⲉⲙ and ⲛ is added as:

ⲫⲉ, heaven	ⲣⲉⲙⲛ-ⲫⲉ, heavenly
phe	remn-phe
ⲕⲁϩⲓ, earth	ⲣⲉⲙⲛ-ⲕⲁϩⲓ, earthly
kahi	remn-kahi
ⲏⲓ, house	ⲣⲉⲙⲛ-ⲏⲓ, domestic
aei	remn-aei
ⲭⲏⲙⲓ, Egypt	ⲣⲉⲙⲛ-ⲭⲏⲙⲓ, an Egyptian
Khaemi	remn-Khaemi

1 nuk pa ba en ta χat āāt

2 ta ḥemt en paif sen āa

Coptic and Hieroglyphics

1- I am the soul of the womb great (great womb).
2- The wife of the brother elder (elder brother)

Glyph	Copt	
nuk	ⲁⲛⲟⲕ	anok, I
pa	ⲡⲉ	pe, the (masculine sing.)
ba	ⲃⲁⲓ	bai, soul
n	ⲛ	n, of
ta	ϯ	ti, the (feminine sing.)
khat	ϧⲏⲧ	khaet, womb, body
aat	ⲁⲓⲁⲓ	aiai, elder, great
hemt	ϩⲓⲙⲉ	hime, wife, woman
paif	ⲡⲉϥ	pef, his
sen	ⲥⲟⲛ	son, brother

    p   pa   ta   na   nan

The Coptic article is used before nouns and their infixes. As indicated above, it has changed little from the hieroglyphics.

Definite Article

ⲠⲒ, Ⲡ, Ⲯ	Ⲧ, Ⲑ, ϯ	ⲚⲒ, Ⲛ, ⲚⲈⲚ
pi, p, ph	t, th, ti	ni, n, nen
(masc. sing.)	(fem. sing.)	(masc. + fem. plural)

Indefinite Article

ⲞⲨ	ϨⲀⲚ
ou	han
(masc. + fem sing.)	(masc. + fem. plural)

Example of the Coptic use of the article;

ⲏⲓ, house
aei

   ⲡⲓ-ⲏⲓ, the house
   pi-aei
   ⲛⲓ-ⲏⲓ, the houses
   ni-aei
   ⲟⲩ-ⲏⲓ, a house
   ou-aei
   ϩⲁⲛ-ⲏⲓ, houses
   han-aei

ⲥⲏϥⲓ, sword
saefi

   ϯ-ⲥⲏϥⲓ, the sword
   ti-saefi
   ⲛⲓ-ⲥⲏϥⲓ, the swords
   ni-saefi
   ⲟⲩ-ⲥⲏϥⲓ, a sword
   ou-saefi
   ϩⲁⲛ-ⲥⲏϥⲓ, swords
   han-saefi

ⲃⲁⲕⲓ, city
baki

   ⲑ-ⲃⲁⲕⲓ, the city
   th-baki
   ⲛⲓ-ⲃⲁⲕⲓ, the cities
   ni-baki
   ⲟⲩ-ⲃⲁⲕⲓ, a city
   ou-baki
   ϩⲁⲛ-ⲃⲁⲕⲓ, cities
   han-baki

When compared with its parent hieroglyphics, the Coptic personal pronouns appear almost unchanged.

           I   We

anok, anak, anag   anon, anan

Second Person Singular

You masculine   You feminine

athok, ntok   ntho, ne

Second Person Plural

You masculine   You feminine

nthoten, noten   thten

Third Person Singular

Him   Her

nthof, ntof   nthos

Third Person Plural

They, Them

nthou, nou, ntoou

Pronoun infixes and suffixes of the hieroglyphics are used extensively in the Coptic. These are often used in place of the personal and possessive pronouns, and are affixed to words.

Coptic Infixes

a, (a) my   ⲉⲛ, (en) our

ⲉⲕ, (ek) you, yours   ⲧⲉⲛ, (ten) yours

ⲉ, (e) " fem.
ⲟⲩ, (ou) "

ⲉϥ, (ef) his   ⲟⲩ, their
ⲉⲥ, (es) her

Suffixes

ⲓ, ⲧ	- ⲕ, ⳓ	ϯ, ⲉ, ⲓ	- ϥ, ⲥ
i, t	k, g	ti, e, i	f, s
me, to me	- you, masculine	you feminine	- him, her

ⲛ, ⲉⲛ	- ⲉⲛ, ⲧⲉⲛ	- ⲟⲩ, ⲁⲩ, ⲉ, ⲁ ⲏⲩ ⲥⲟⲩ
n, en	en, ten	ou, au, e, a, aeu, sou
us, to us	- you, to you plural	- them, to them

Examples:
ϣнρι, son

ⲡ-ⲁ-ϣнρι, my son
ⲡ-ⲉⲕ-ϣнρι, thy son
ⲡ-ⲉϥ-ϣнρι, his son
ⲡ-ⲉⲥ-ϣнρι, her son

ⲡ-ⲉⲛ-ϣнρι, our son
ⲡ-ⲉⲧⲉⲛ-ϣнρι, your son
ⲡ-ⲟⲩ-ϣнρι, their son

Pronoun Suffixes are used in place of the Infixes, and are placed on the end of Coptic pronouns. These are also used in the hieroglyphics.

ι, ϯ	me, my	ⲛ, ⲉⲛ	us, ours
ⲕ,	thee, thy	ⲉⲛ, ⲧⲉⲛ	they, their
ϯ, ⲉ, ι,	thee, thy (f)		
ϥ,	him, his	ⲟⲩ	they, theirs
ⲥ,	she, her		

Examples:
ϫⲱ, head

ϫⲱ-ι, my head
ϫⲱ-ⲕ, thy head
ϫⲱ-ϯ, thy head (f)

ϫⲱ-ⲛ, our head
ϫⲱ-ⲧⲉⲛ, your head

ϫⲱ-ⲟⲩ, their head

66

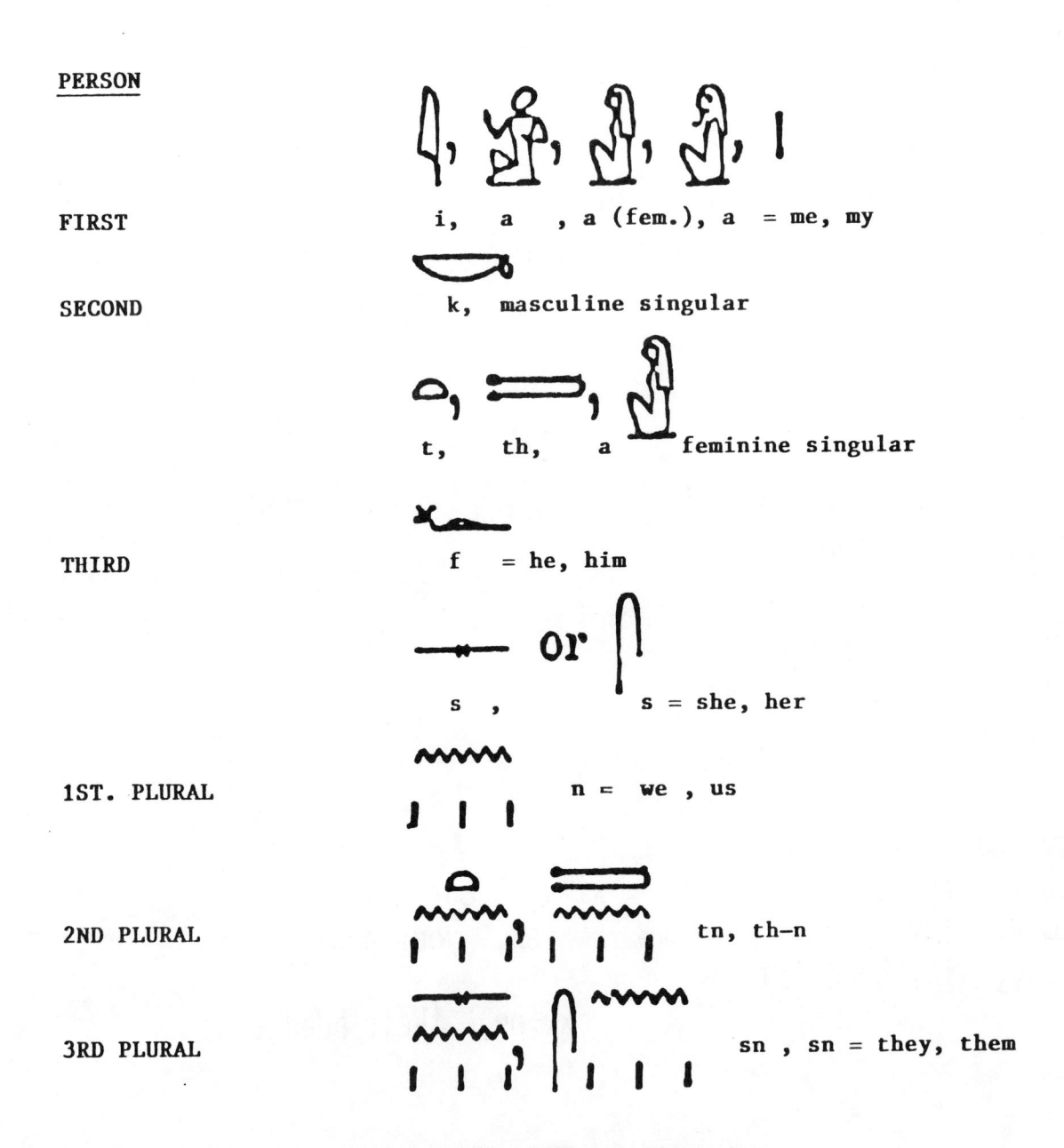

PERSON		
FIRST	𓇋, 𓀀, 𓁐, 𓁑, 𓏤	i, a, a (fem.), a = me, my
SECOND	𓎡	k, masculine singular
	𓏏, 𓍿, 𓁐	t, th, a — feminine singular
THIRD	𓆑	f = he, him
	─ or 𓊃	s, s = she, her
1ST. PLURAL	𓈖 / 𓏪	n = we, us
2ND PLURAL	𓏏𓈖𓏪 , 𓍿𓈖𓏪	tn, th-n
3RD PLURAL	𓊃𓈖𓏪 , 𓋴𓈖𓏪	sn, sn = they, them

HIEROGLYPHIC PRONOUN SUFFIXES

„	2. m.	[hieroglyphs]	ENTEK, ENTUK
„	2. f.	[hieroglyphs]	ENTET, ENTUT
„	3. m.	[hieroglyphs]	ENTEF, ENTUF
„	3. f.	[hieroglyphs]	ENTES, ENTUS.
Plur.	1.	(wanting)	
„	2.	[hieroglyphs]	ENTETEN, ENTUTEN
„	3.	[hieroglyphs]	ENTESEN, ENTUSEN.

Some Coptic Possessive Pronouns are formed from the Personal Pronouns by the addition of "т" after the first "ⲛ", and are found in the hieroglyphics.

ⲛⲁⲕ, to thee	ⲛⲧⲁⲕ, thine (yours)	NTAK
ⲛⲁϥ, to him	ⲛⲧⲁϥ, his	NTAF
ⲛⲁⲥ, to her	ⲛⲧⲁⲥ, hers	NTAS
ⲛⲁⲛ, to us	ⲛⲧⲁⲛ, ours	NTAN
ⲛⲱⲧⲉⲛ, to you	ⲛⲧⲱⲧⲉⲛ, yours	NTUTEN
ⲛⲱⲟⲩ, to them	ⲛⲧⲱⲟⲩ, theirs	NTU

The hieroglyphics form was mistaken by Egyptologist as a form of the personal pronouns. However the Coptic equivalent demonstrates that they are possessive pronouns.

1		rex-á	I know
2		nehem-k	thou deliverest
3		tef-t	thou speakest
4		sát-f	he cuts
5		qem-	she finds
6		ári-n	we do
7		mit-ten	ye die
8		xeper-sen	they become.

Verb Suffix

Person	Glyph	Coptic	
1- 1st person singular	a	ⲁ	a
2- 2nd person singular	k	ⲕ	k
3- 2nd person singular feminine	t	ⲧ	t
4- 3rd person masculine singular	f	ϥ	f
5- 3rd person feminine singular	s	ⲥ	s
6- 1st person plural	n	ⲉⲛ	en
7- 2nd person plural	ten	ⲧⲉⲛ	ten
8- 3rd person plural	sen	ⲥⲟⲩ	sou

ta   ohae   ari   un   au

Auxiliary Verb

Glyph	Coptic		Meaning
tae	ϯ	ti	to give
ohae	ⲁϩⲏ	ahae	to stand
	ⲁϩⲉ	ahe	
	ⲁϩⲁ	aha	
	ⲟϩⲉ	ohe	
	ⲱϩⲉ	ooaee	
ari	ⲉⲓⲣⲉ	eire	to do
	ⲉⲣ	er	
	ⲓⲣⲓ	iri	
un	ⲟⲩⲟⲛ	ouon	to be
au	ⲟⲩⲱϩ	ouooh	to be

Hathor-head designs. Painted tomb ceiling. Thebes. XVIIIth Dynasty.

Greek Philosophy.

"Greek Philosophy", as a term coined by modern western historians, is a misnomer, in that the Greeks who were alleged to have formulated it, derived it from the ancient African "Mysteries" of the Nile Valley Civilization. The ancient people who lived in the area now known as Greece, were not a homogenous group of people as those who are Greek today. In Coptic, the only term used to characterize the people who modern historians call Greek, in translation is "Ionian". Pictographically expressed and delineated phonically through the hieroglyphics, the term is "Ounu, Ounnua", from which derived the Coptic "Oueeienin or Oueinin" for Ionian, inhabitants of Asia Minor. Ionia was also a stronghold of the ancient African (Egyptian) Mystery Schools, and until the Persian invasion of Egypt, was a subject of Egypt.

As a "Secret Order", entry into the African "Mystery System" was through initiation and pledge of secrecy. The "Philosophical Schools" of the Order expressed ancient African philosophical thought. The teachings were common among the "Subordinate Schools" or "Lodges" of the colonies which had their "Mother-Grand-Lodge" or Lodges on the main land of Africa, from which subordinate "Grand Lodges" were chartered.

From the Persian invasion to the invasion of Alexander the Great, Greeks entered African "Philosophical Schools" and were initiated into the higher "Mysteries". From Ionia, came Thales and his associates Anaximender and Anaximenes, came Xenophanes, Parenides, Zeno, and Melissus, who migrated to Elea, Italy, and later to Greece, also Heraclitus, Empedocles, Anaxagoras, and Democritus, who studied Physics and went to Greece to teach, all went to Africa (Egypt) for extended and/or final studies in the "Mysteries". Not unlike the others, Herodotus was also schooled in Africa, where he entered into the "Mysteries", studying history, science, philosophy, religion, magic, medicine, law, government..,etc. According to Hermodorus, at 28 Plato went to school in Africa (Egypt) to learn the "Mysteries", as did countless other Greeks, for Africa was the center of learning at that time.

Aristotle, with the aid of Alexander's chief general, Soter (Ptolemy I) and soldiers gained access to the Library and other repositories of the "Mysteries System" in Egypt, removing many works. It is believed that Aristotle placed his name as author on many of these works. This would account for the ridiculous number of publications ascribed to him, that in fact no single human being could have written in a lifetime. Some scholars also believe that other materials from the Library were sent to friends of Aristotle who in turn claimed authorship.

The Greek authorities, at the time rejected the African philosophical concepts, learned by those educated in the "Mysteries". Those so learned were accused and condemned for teaching a "foreign philosophy", by furthering the study and investigation into astronomy and geometry, and introducing African divinities to the Greeks. Those educators were persecuted, imprisoned, and exiled by the Greek authorities. Anaxogoras was imprisoned and exiled, Socrates was executed, Plato was sold into slavery, and Aristotle was indited and exiled. Obviously, those educated into the "Mysteries", and who propagated their learning to the early Greeks were classed as undesirable by the ancient Greek authorities, for teaching a philosophy that was not Greek and therefore "foreign". The persecuted educators should be given credit for the start of a movement that would civilize all of Europe. Modern western historians later glorified these educators and coined their philosophy, "Greek Philosophy".

According to Didorus Siculus, many Greeks visited ancient Egypt for learning, and won fame for their learning. From the records of their sacred books, Egyptian priest recount visits from; Orpheus, Musaeus, Melampus, Daedalus, and Lycurgus of Sparta, later by Solon of Athens and the philosopher Plato, and also Pythagoras of Samos and the mathematician Eudoxus (also a noted astronomer and geographer of Cnidus) as well as Democritus of Abdera and Oenopides of Chios.

Orpheus, says Diodorus, brought from Egypt most of his mystic ceremonies. The rites of Osiris is the same as that of Dionysus, and that of Isis very similar to that of Demeter, the names alone having been interchanged.

He further states that many of the fantastic conceptions of the Greeks were figments of their imagination, through the introduction of imitations of Egyptian funeral customs. He sites Hermes as a Egyptian reproduction. Melampus, also brought from Egypt, the Egyptian rites celebrated by the Greeks in the name of Dionysus, the myth of Cronus and the war with the Titans. Daedalus copied the maze of the Labyrinth. Myths which relate about the dalliances of Zeus and Hera and their journey to Ethiopia, as contained in the Homeric passage (14th Book), are of Egyptian origin. Lycurgus, Plato, and Solon, incorporated many Egyptian customs in their legislation. Pythagoras learned from Egypt, teachings of the gods, his geometrical propositions and theory of numbers, as well as the transmigration of the soul into every living thing. Democritus of Abdera (so-called author of the atomic theory), spent five years among the Egyptians and was instructed in many matters relating to astrology. Oenopides likewise studied in Egypt, studying astrology and learned the orbit of the sun, so too Eudoxus. Telecles and Theodorus, the sons of Rhoecus, who were sculptors, also journeyed among the Egyptians.

The "pre-Socratic" philosophers learned and taught the ancient African thoughts learned in the Egyptian schools. Thales from the early Ionian schools who supposedly lived about 620-546 B.C. taught that water was the source of all living things and that all things were full of God. This coincide with the concept of "Nu and Nut" who personified the cosmic waters of primordial matter from which the Deity came into being, and from whose Being all else evolved. That all things are full of God, is confirmed by their evolution from the Deity whose matter is from the All. Throughout the hieroglyphics the term "ntr" or "neter" is used to define the essence of the Deity, found in all things by virtue of their evolution from it (the Deity).

Anaximander (610 B.C.) of Miletus, is credited with the teachings that the origin of all things is the "Infinite" or the "Unlimited". The concept of the infinite or unlimited is equivalent to the modern ideas about space and the mythological idea of the "Chaos". Actually this idea is not very different from the hydro-genesis concept, in that the primordial cosmic waters were boundless or unlimited. Anaximenes who died 528 B.C., also from Miletus subscribed to the teaching that all things originated from the air. This does not contradict the belief in the primordial matter, rather it supposes that its genesis is from the air.

It is written that Pythagoras (528 B.C.) from the Aegean Island of Samos was put through a cleansing rite before he could obtain entry to the Egyptian temple. Part of the rite mandated that Pythagoras undergo the traditional African circumcision procedure, which he did. From his African education he came away with the following understanding, which he taught;

(1)- Transmigration
(2)- Union of Opposition
(3)- Supreme Good
(4)- Purification

Transmigration

Dealing with the immortality of the soul and its salvation, transmigration contends that the physical body is the tomb of the soul and earthly life is death. It further contends that the imprisonment of the soul in the body is a contamination that can only be rectified by an infinite series of reincarnations from the body of one animal to another, until such time that the contamination is purged. This infinite series of reincarnations are common to all souls. Salvation is obtained when the soul is free of the cycle of birth, death, and rebirth. In this liberation the soul acquires her perfection which qualifies her to join the immortal collective of the company of God, dwelling therein forever.

The Union Of Opposition

Universal harmony was believed to be the product of the unity of opposition, through the compromise of the extremes. This unification of opposition is expressed in numbers whose elements consist of odd and even. The even being unlimited and the odd being limited, while the product of both is the unity and harmony. Similarly, harmony is obtained in the union of positive and negative, male and female, or the material and immaterial.

Supreme Good

The supreme good is obtained through the domination of the higher nature over the lower nature of human being, leading to a state of Godlyness, which is the harmony resulting from virtue. This was the motivation behind the moral precepts written in the hieroglyphics.

Purification

In addition to virtue, the cultivation of intellect through the pursuit of scientific knowledge and discipline of the body, facilitates harmony and purification of the soul. From the doctrine of the "Three Lives", e.g., lovers of wealth, lovers of honor, and lovers of wisdom, it is determined that the lovers of wisdom are on the correct path to the final salvation of the soul.

Interwoven into the Egyptian teachings were cosmological doctrines which stated that the entire universe was an arrangement of numbers, and the characteristic of any object was the number by which it was represented. The universe was represented by the perfect number 10, which is the common base system of modern numeration. The boundless or limitless space is thus in proportionate distribution as to facilitate a harmonious universe, each component receiving its proper share. Thus, all forms can be represented by a mathematical expression. This doctrine appeared in Plato as the "Theory of Ideas". The center of the universe was conceived as a fire around which heavenly bodies were fixed in their spheres and all around, a peripheral fire. Motion of the heavenly bodies were regulated in the velocity, which produced the harmony of the spheres.

The Writing Revolution, Prelude to Biblical Literature

The writing revolution forged by the early ancestors is responsible for the sacred literature passed on through the Bible. Moses, who is recognized as the father of Hebrew culture, reached the rank of priest in Egypt. In the Biblical texts, it is stated that Moses was found floating along the river in a basket by the king of Egypt's daughter, and raised by her. His name in Egyptian mean "water son", from "mu" (water) and "sa" (son). He rose to prominence and formed a nation. Moses (Musa) developed a culture and a code of conduct for his nation. Acts chapter 7 verse 22 of the Biblical Texts state that Moses was learned in all the wisdom of the ancient Egyptians. At this time in human history, Africa was the center of all arts and sciences. Moses applied his knowledge learned in Africa to create a literature and a culture for the mixed multitude of people that comprised his nation. It stands to reason that from the revolutionary system of recording human speech created by the Africans in Egypt, an industrious individual could, with modification, develop another system using the same format of the parent system. Thus, the similarity between the Hebrew alphabet, and the corresponding culture, to that of the Egyptians can only be attributed to the derivation of the former from the latter (the Egyptians). It is then understandable, why the Hebrew alphabet and much of the culture expressed in the Books of Moses coincide with the Egyptians. One need only compare the Hebrew alphabet with its pictographic parent, the African hieroglyphics.

Ancient Egyptian records to date, do not mention an exodus of Hebrews as described in the books of Moses.

Manetho, an Egyptian historian who wrote about 250 B.C, and whose lost works can only be gathered from authors who quote from him, recorded an interesting account of a group of people expelled from Egypt. In a narrative from the works of a writer named Josephus, Manetho is quoted as follows:

A certain king Amenophis, son of Paapis was told by his priest, that he must rid the land of the unclean in order to receive blessing from the gods (orishas) of the land. He (the king) gathered all the lepers and those suffering from "white sickness" (80,000 in all) and cast them in the stone quarries. There were some learned priest among them. The priest of the king believed that casting learned priest among the others in the quarries, would not be met with favor by the gods (orishas), and would justify others helping them in their plight. So the priest prophesied, that the lepers would rule for 13 years.

After a time the king removed the lepers and the sufferers of "white sickness" from the quarries to the town of Apris. In this town, they became organized and appointed a priest named "Osarsiph" as their leader, and swore to obey him. Osarsiph established as their first law, that they should not pay homage to any of the gods and should not abstain from the sacred meats of the Egyptians, rather feed upon it without regard. They were instructed to associate only with their co-conspirators.

The parallel between Menetho's story and the exodus narrated in the bible is too inviting to forego discussion. Osarsiph, in Menetho's story, like Moses in the biblical texts, established as a first law, that his people not worship any of the gods. Osarsiph and his followers were removed to the town of Apris (Apis, Avaris), in the delta area of Egypt. Apris was also known as Pelusium, which was Pi-Ramessu prior, the town Rameses in the bible. Rameses was the delta capitol of the XIX Dynasty. Oddly enough, Osarsiph and Moses are tied to the same geographical spot. Moses met Pharoah at Rameses, and his exodus took place from this point. The king removed Osarsiph and his people to the town of Apis, which we've identified with Rameses. Compilers of history naturally replace city or town names with their modern equivalent, as Apis (Avaris) for Ramases by Manetho.

Whether Menetho grafted his story from the Hebrew one, or obtained it from official Egyptian records, we cannot truly say. More than likely Menetho's story is probably the Egyptian version of an expulsion of people.

The Inscription of the Creation

The ancient creation story written in the African pictographic script, state that the Beginning was Primordial Matter or Abyss. This Matter was the cosmic roots of All that existed, past and future. It was neither male nor female, but was a complete entity composed of the duality of all nature, and therefore both male and female, as Nu and Nut or Nau and Nen. The dynamics of its darkness, perhaps can be best understood by what we know about the "black hole" in astronomy. It was the "Deep", and a cosmic water of generations. Coming forth from the darkness of this Primordial Abyss (Nu) was the firing energy of activation, in the form of light, called "Khpr-Rae". Then there was the dryness, "Shu", which separated the waters above from the waters below (Tefnut). From this the dry land of the earth (Geb) was formed, and the waters (Nut) on it that gathered together became the seas. The sun (Rae) was the greater light over the earth, and the moon (Khuti) was its lesser light.

Nu and the feminine counter part Nut, denote a primordial fluid, from whose essence all that exist is derived, and is contained in all things. It is the indestructible matter of the universe. This word has survived in Coptic, prefixed with the masculine article and suffixed with the feminine article to maintain the original duality of the concept, to form the word "God" (ϕ-ⲛⲟⲩ-ϯ). Khpru is a word that mean to generate, create, or bring to form. When attached to the word rae (sun), it implies the generation of the light or the creation of the light. The title to the creation story contained in the Book of Pylons is "The Book of Knowledge of the Creation of the Light". The name "Shu", in translation mean dry, empty, parched or withered, and is the second deity formed in the ancient Egyptian creation. Genesis makes use of the word "firmament", "expanse" is used in the Torah. Shu is the sky deity, and Genesis 1:8 says "And God called the firmament Heaven", the Torah reads "God called the expanse Sky". Genesis 1:6 state "Let there be a firmament in the midst of the waters and let it divide the waters from the waters". The initial water is the primordial Deep cosmic water of generations, Nu. Genesis 1:7 tell us that the firmament separated the water above it from the water below it. The second deity of the Egyptian creation was Tefnut, which is moisture, as oppose to dryness of Shu. Thus Shu as dryness partitioned the waters, and Tefnut came into being. From one deity we now have a trinity. In fact the Egyptian texts reveal that the Creator was alone, and that from one deity three deities came into being. Continuing on, Geb or Seb and Nut are formed from the dryness (Shu) and the moisture (Tefnut). Seb or Geb is the earth deity, and Nut is the gathering of the waters on the earth, i.e. the seas. What we have here written in hieroglyphics is a overly simplified interpretation of a complex theory of a genesis.

Pictographic writing expressed complicated concepts, ideas, and theories. Its system of symbolism served as a quick reference for the initiate. The science in the dynamics of the universe was expressed in a simple African fashion. We should not, however, think for one moment that we could completely decipher in one or two generations, a system and ideas that developed over tens of thousands of of years of human historical experiences. Granted, we have made significant advances in understanding what has been handed down from the ancestors of the human family, we still have more to learn. At best, we have scratched the surface, in terms of understanding what the ancients perceived, and their source of documentation. Although the story of creation or the generation of life is spelled out so simple, we may not appreciate to the fullest, the knowledge required to simplify complexity. The ancient concept of the duality of all things is tied to the creation in the image of nature. Thus, if nature is dual as mandated by this formula then every aspect of nature has its counter-part, acting in opposition in a unified matter. This unity of opposition is the dynamics of motion in nature. The following are deities in their dual form, male and female, and are personifications of phases, aspects or properties of the Primordial Matter.

Nu, Nut	= Primordial Watery Abyss
Hehu, Hehut	= Light
Kerkui, Kerkuit	= Darkness, before and after day
Gerh, Gerhet	= Darkness, inactive in the day

The first book Genesis, in the Torah (T) and the Bible (B), we see a reproduction of the same story without the pictographic symbolism of the hieroglyphics.

Biblical Reference = B, Torah Reference = T

Genesis 1:

B   1- In the beginning God created the heaven and earth.

T   1- When God began to create (In the Beginning God created) the heaven and earth

B   2- And the earth was without form, and void: and darkness was upon the face of the deep. And the spirit of God moved upon the face of the waters.

T   2- The earth being un-formed and void with darkness over the surface of the deep and a wind (spirit of God) from God sweeping over the water

        Nu, Nut, the Deep

B   3- And God said Let there be Light and there was Light

T   3- God said Let there be Light and there was Light

        Khpr-Rae, the creation of the Light

        (Hehu, Hehut- male and female aspect of fire or the light)

B   4- And God saw the Light that it was good: and God divided the Light from the darkness

T   4- God saw that the Light was good, and God separated the Light from the darkness

        (Kerkui, Kerkuit- male and female aspect of darkness proceeding and following day)

B   5- And God called the Light, Day and the darkness He called Night, and the evening and the morning was the first day.

T   5- And God called the Light, Day, and the darkness He called night. And there was evening and there was morning, a first day. (one day)

Gerh, Gerhet

B 6- And God said let there be a a firmament in the midst of the waters, and let it divide the waters from the waters.

T 6- God said Let there be an expanse in the midst of the water, that it may separate water from water (Shu, dryness, separated Tefnut, wetness)

Shu, firmament, sky

B 7- And God made the firmament, and divided the waters which were under the firmament from the waters which were above the firmament: and it was so

T 7- God made the expanse, and it separated the water which was below the expanse from the water which above the expanse. And it was so.

Tefnut = waters above heaven

B 8- And God called the firmament Heaven, and the evening and the morning were the second day

T 8- God called the expanse Sky. And there was evening and there was morning, a second day.

Shu = heaven = firmament

B 9- And God said Let the waters under the heaven be gathered together unto one place, and Let the dry land appear, and it was so.

T 9- God said Let the water below the Sky be gathered into one area, that the dry land may appear. And it was so.

Nut = water below heaven

B 10-And God called the dry land Earth: and the gathering together of the waters called He Seas. And God

T   saw that it was good.

T   10-God called the dry land Earth, and the gathering of waters He called Seas. And He saw that it was good.
(Dry land, Geb or Seb, and the Seas Nut)
Geb = Earth
Nut = Seas

The wide range of variation between Jewish populations in their physical characteristics and the diversity of the gene frequencies of their blood groups render any unified ethnic classification for them a contradiction in terms. It appears that Jews are a religious sect composed of ethnic elements acquired by proselytism and intermarriage during their migration in various parts of the world.

Miscegenation was a integral part of Judaic history as evidenced by the Bible. We find, Asia Minor, Syria and Palestinc of Biblical times, populated by various ethnic elements. The Amorites, who were blondes, dolichocephalic, and tall, lived in the area; the Hittites, a dark complexioned ethnic group; the black Cushites and many others typified the various ethnic elements in the region and with whom the ancient Hebrews intermarried, as testified by the Bible. Abraham, cohabited with Hagar, an Egyptian; Joseph married Asenath, the daughter of an Egyptian priest; Moses married the black skinned Zipporah, the Midianite; Samson, the Jewish hero was a Philistine; King David's mother was a Mobite and King Solomon's mother was a Hittite. Exodus from the blackland of Egypt with 600,000 Israelites, included a mixed multitude from Egypt. The Chinese Jews of Kai-Feng, the dark skinned Yemenite Jews, the Berber Jews of the Sahara and the black Falasha of Ethiopia are all examples of the ethnic diversity of the people who today are called Jews. Never the less, the development of writing and historical inscriptions connects Judaism to Africa via the Egyptian Empire.

Therefore, the present followers of Judaism are culturally tied to ancient Egypt, through the maintenance of the literature thereof.

The largest groups of people who follow Judaism today can be placed in two divisions, Sephardim and Ashkenazim.

The Sephardim (Sepharad in Hebrew) are descendants of the Judaic followers who since antiquity, lived in Spain until they were expelled at the end of the 15th century. They settled in the countries bordering the Mediterranean, the Balkans, and to a lesser extent in Western Europe. Ladino, a Spanish-Hebrew mixture, written in Hebrew characters, was the spoken dialect of the Sephardim. Preserved in this dialect were their traditions and religious rites. In the 1960's, the number of Sephardim was estimated at 500,000. The Ashkenazim, at the same period, were numbered at about 11,000,000. Thus in common parlance, "Jew" is practically synonymous with Ashkenazi Jew. The term is misleading, for the Hebrew word Ashkenaz was, in medieval rabbinical literature, applied to Germany.

It should be mentioned that Ashkenaz of the Bible refers to a people living in the vicinity of Mount Ararat and Armenia. The name occured in Genesis 10, 3 and in I Chronicles 1, 6, as one of the sons of Gomer, a son of Japheth. Ashkenaz is also a brother of Togarmah (and a nephew of Magog) whom the Khazars, according to their King Joseph, claim as their ancestor. The Khazars were a people of Turkish stock, and their land occupied a strategic key at the vital gateway between the Black Sea and the Caspian. This area acted as a buffer protecting the kingdom of Byzantine against invasion from barbarian tribesmen from the north, and blocked the Arab invasion in its most devastating early stages, thus preventing the Muslim conquest of Eastern Europe. The Khazars were converted to Judaism at some point in their history, and Judaism became the official religion of the ruling strata of their society. It is not certain what became of the followers of of Judaism in Khazaria after its fall in the twelfth or thirteenth century. However, late medieval Khazar settlements are mentioned in Crimea, Ukraine, Hungry, Poland, and Lithuania. This fragmented piece of information suggest that there was a migration of Khazar tribes and communities into those regions of Eastern Europe, mainly Russia and Poland, where, at the dawn of the Modern Age, the greatest concentration of Jews were found. This has led several historians to conjecture that a substantial part, and perhaps the majority of the eastern Jews (world Jewry), might be of Khazar origin, as opposed to Semitic origin. A. Poliak, a Professor of Medieval Jewish History at Tel Aviv University published his book entitled "Khazaria" in Hebrew in 1944 and a second addition is 1951, and called for a new approach in understanding the descent of modern Jewry from the Khazars.

The Khazars conversion to Judaism, didn't occur over night. They had been acquainted with Judaism and its religious observances for at least a century before the conversion. Khazaria became a natural haven for the periodic exodus of Jews under the Byzantine rule, threatened by forced conversion and other pressures. Persecution of Jews in Byzantine started with Justinian I (527-565 AD), and assumed particularly vicious forms under Heraclius in the 7th century, Leo III in the 8th, Basil and Leo IV in the 9th, Romanus in the 10th century.

Leo III, who ruled during the two decades immediately preceding the Khazar conversion to Judaism, attempted to end the tolerated status of Jews at one blow, by ordering that all Jewish subjects be baptized. Although the implementation of the order seemed to have been ineffective, it led to the flight of a considerable number of Jews from Byzantine.

Modern scholars obtained their information on the Khazars from Arab, Byzantine, Russian and Hebrew sources. Dr. Antal Bartha, a Hungarian, in his book "The Magyars Society in the Eight and Ninth Centuries", made reference to the Khazars, as they once ruled the Hungarians. An impressive and more recent publication by Arthur Koestler entitled "The Thirteenth Tribe", gives clear and convincing evidence of the connection between the Khazars and Judaism in Eastern Europe.

Conclusion

More than just an African invention, the advent of writing was the greatest human achievement, for it made all other achievements possible. As such it is the heritage of the human race. Anthropologist have theorized an African genesis of the human animal for more than a half a century. Africans are among the earliest people mentioned in the creation story of the first book of the Bible. Thus, it was not by mistake or coincidence that those who study ancient bones began their search in Africa to the southeast, and found the oldest human remains. Perhaps there is some validity to the biblical reference to a garden Eden to the east where the earliest human ancestor is reported to have taken up residence. Modern microbiologist through the study of what is known as mitochondrial DNA passed on only by a women, slightly changed over millions of years by periodic mutations, have experimentally determined that all of humanity came forth from the same kind of African woman. Implications are that Africans are a precursor people, and it only stands to logical reasoning that early writing which forged civilization was born there. Apparently there is but one race on this earth, and that is the human race. For many who have been taught or socialized that other humans were inferior and therefore warrant hatred, and others who have learned to accept their presumed inferiority might find a disturbing reflection in the mirror. One might see the very person hated the most. No one wins when the price is hate. Accepting the brother and sisterhood of humanity removes the need for any individual group claim to human scientific and technological developments. The story of the development of the Egyptian hieroglyphics and the corresponding literature is a story of the human will to grow and learn about itself and the garden earth in which it found itself.

Like a child born into the world, from the dark abyss of the woman's womb, who through distance from that event has lost all conscious recollection of the primordial abode in which it spent 9 months in development, we as humans through the great span of time from our early beginnings have lost all conscious recollection of our most ancient past. Surely at one point we knew from whence we came, and how we have changed into different ethnic groups of many hues and speaking different languages. This is, however, no longer a matter of conscious record. Information pertaining to early beginnings of the human animal is permanently stored and recorded within the matter that transcribes our biological being, the genes. Through genetic studies, modern science concedes to the fact that in actuality, there is only one race on earth and that is the human one. The earliest beginnings of the modern human animal can be traced to the continent of Africa, and at least to an African woman. Such that, when one speak of people of African descent, in the most broader sense this reference is to the whole of humanity. The distance that time places between any event does not render that event insignificant. That the human animal has forgotten its origin from black skinned people, as a result of the antiquity of that event, does not erase this fact from history nor make it less important. The perpetuation of so-called racial hatred of blacker skinned individuals, inaccurate demonstrations of their inferiority, contrived on the basis of their skin tone, is of itself a hatred of one's own reflection in the mirror.

Biology is a science which studies the totality of earthly life. With a better understanding of human genes and how they cause a whole being to be formed from infinitely many predetermined blue prints, an understanding of our early beginnings can be realized. Deoxyribo-Nucleaic Acid (DNA) is found in the nucleus of every cell and is the biochemical blue print for every detail that characterize a living organism. Basically, it is inherited from both the mother and father organism. Within every cell is a structure called the mitochondria, which provides a mechanism or mechanisms to facilitate the energy needs of the cell, without which no cell could live. Science learned in 1960 that the mitochondria contained genes. Family trees could be traced through the mitochondria, as the genes in it are only inherited from the mother. DNA from the nucleus of the cell inherited from both mother and father changes every generation. Mitochondrial DNA (mtDNA), however, solely inherited from the mother is virtually unchanged except as a result of random mutation, approximated at about 2% to 4% every million years. An examination of present day mtDNA would allow scientists to point back to a female or female type from which it (mtDNA) was derived since its origins are solely maternal.

In order to get large samples of body tissue for mtDNA studies, scientists obtained baby placenta from 147 women. Placentas were obtained from American women with ancestry from Africa, Europe, the Middle East, Asia, in addition from women of New Guinea, and the Aboriginal women of Australia. In view of what we know about mtDNA what result might we expect? First, the fact that the mtDNA remains unchanged for long periods of time except for selective mutations, should determine which group of people represented by the women are the oldest group. We would expect to see a greater degree of diversity in the mtDNA of the older group due to the effect of selective mutation as a result of antiquity. Second, we would hope to see a pattern that would reflect a difference between the groups. The result of the investigation in fact demonstrated that there was a greater diversity in the mtDNA of the women exclusively African, and less diversity between the other groups, including the African American group. The exclusively African group had accumulated more mutations and was therefore more diversified because it had been around longer. Apparently the DNA tree began in Africa, and at some point emigrated, splitting off to form other branches of DNA, carrying it to the rest of the world. Overall the genetic differences between the various groups, although clear was surprisingly small. That is, there wasn't much difference between the so-called races. It appeared that as a specie, humans were much more closely related than any other vertebrate or mammalian species. This led scientist to believe that the human specie is relatively young, showing few genetic differences among cultures, that would have been manifested if more time were allowed. All humans can thus be traced to a single group of women, who for want of a better name was called "Eve" by the scientists who did the study, and who passed her genetic mtDNA through the birth of daughters to successive generations.

Genetically it was demonstrated that African people are the oldest people on earth. Fossils of modern humans dating 100,000 years old have been found in Africa. The diversity of the various stocks of African people and the languages that owe their diversity and change to antiquity, are other indicators that point to the fact that Africans are the oldest humans. Contrary to modern stereotype images of Africans propagated through western literature and mass media, the greatest common denominator among all Africans is not their anatomical characteristics but only their skin color, as black or dark brown. No single stock of African people can be used as an example to represent all of Africa.

For example there are indigenous stocks of Africans who are among the tallest people in the world to those that represent the shortest people in the world. There are those with thick protruding lips to those with thinner fleshy lips. Hair types are also numerous, ranging from tightly curled and short to wavy and long. In the eastern region of Africa we find stocks that have sharp features almost comparable to Europeans, and it is reasonable to believe that Europeans may be descendant from them. Perhaps nowhere else on earth can we find such a linguistical diversity as shown in the peoples of Africa. These diversities and broad changes in human populations require tens of thousands of years to become manifested. Skin color is the single factor held in common among indigenous African people, and that is a minor adaptation to the heat and light of the sun, requiring only a few thousand years of evolution to change.

Bone specialist suggest that modern humans are about one million years old, but the molecular clock theory introduced by the mtDNA specialist who suggest a 2% to 4% selective mutation rate over a million year period, calculated an earlier date. Scientist from the University of California at Berkely looked at the most distant branches of the family tree, the DNA types most different from one another to determine a time table for modern humans. Working backwards to figure out how many steps it would have taken for those early women's (Eve) DNA to mutate into these different types, they assumed that these mutations occurred at a regular rate, a controversial assumption that might be in error, but which has been supported by some human and animal studies. Applying molecular calculus, the Berkely biologist contend that this precursor African female type must have lived about 200,000 years ago (the range is between 140,000 - 290,000 years). This date agrees with the estimate of a team of geneticist led by Douglas Wallace of Emory University. For some scientists this estimated date confirms the fact that modern humans have a more recent history than previously suggested by the bone specialist.

The mighty power released from the splitting of the atom, a power which offers great destructive and constructive potential for humanity as it attempts to prepare itself for a new era, is indicative of the source of energy to which tomorrow world will ultimately depend. The nuclear sciences, and the mathematics tied to it have as its roots, the culture of the Nile Valley Civilization, transferred to the western world through the art of writing. Without the transcription, storage, and radiation of acquired human knowledge as a foundation, civilization would not have reached its current stage of development. It was the cumulative compilation from generations that laid the foundation, and gave acquired knowledge the momentum to continue to grow despite the fact that it changed hands. From literature to science, modern libraries are stocked with a wealth of knowledge that has been passed down from the earliest ancestors. One can hardly read a book or write one for that matter without sharing in that part of history that led to the development of the transcription of human speech, the ancient Egyptian hieroglyphics. From the African civilization inundated by the longest river in the world, a revolution gave birth to the genesis of literature. That genesis was the catalyst to the transformation of world science.

The art of writing is taken for granted. Without the written word, civilization could not have advanced to its current level. In book II of the "Histories" by Herodotus, the priests of Africa reveals to him that they kept records for approximately 11,340 years, of the priests and their sons. Thus, the African hieroglyphics is at least that old. It is uncanny that the language that existed then has descended almost unchanged in the Coptic language, such that the Coptic appear to be merely a mirror reflection of it. At an ancient period of human history this language was a lingua franca, that could lay claim to every major ancient literary work. In addition to the complete Christian Bible, works on the arts and sciences can be found written in the Coptic language. One would wonder, how could such an important language go unnoticed by scholars. The fact of the matter is that it has not gone unnoticed by western scholars. The vast amount of Coptic material recovered remain in research libraries around the world. Incidently, the recovered material merely scratches the surface as far as the vast amount of material actually produced. Its key to deciphering the hieroglyphics is well understood. Some western scholars have attempted to deny Coptic as an African language, just as they have attempted to excise Egypt from the continent of Africa. Their arguments have only succeeded in producing a jumble of intellectual rubbish. Sir E.A.W Budge, the late keeper of the Assyrian and Egyptian Antiquities of the British Museum finally confirmed to western readers that the Egyptians were Africans who spoke an African language. Mr. Budge, despite other shortcomings regarding the ancient Egyptians, certainly hit the mark on this point. He refutes the many arguments by his contemporaries who hoped to define the Coptic as other than African. Mr. Budge also suggested that the interested parties need only examine the languages currently spoken in the eastern Sudan to find similarities between modern African languages and the ancient Egyptians (see Hieroglyphic Dictionary, introduction, Budge). Cheika Anta Diop of the Walaf people of west Africa have also noted similarities between the Walaf of West Africa and the ancient Egyptian language (see Parente genetique des egyptiens pharoniq ue et des langes negres africaines, Diop 1954).

The early denial of the Coptic language by western scholars, in favor of the Greek as the precursor of western literature, served the need of the westerners to carve a world in its own image, boosting its own self esteem and thus forging its upward mobilization. In view of the great advances by the west, it appears that it has proven itself to itself, and the denial and suppression of the facts serve no useful purpose. The stolen legacy must be returned to its origin, Coptic is the African logos of antiquity. The many sororities and fraternaties using so-called Greek letters as logos are in fact using the African logos of antiquity.

APPENDIX

The fact that symbol writing and picture writing are natural, it would only stand to reason that this type of writing was the first. The African hieroglyphics appears not only to have led to the development of the alphabet currently used by modern western nations, but other ancient eastern alphabets, particularly the Hebrew alphabet. If we compare the Hebrew alphabet with some of the symbols of the African hieroglyphics, it becomes readily apparent that there is a mark similarity between them. This leads us to conclude that the Hebrew alphabet, used to record much of the Old Testament bible was derived from the African hieroglyphics. Little is said of Moses, who is considered the father of the Hebrew culture. We do know that Moses was raised by an African woman, and as her own child. Statements in the Bible indicate that Moses was learned in the arts of the Egyptians. Thus it should not be surprising that the Hebrew alphabet favors the hieroglyphics. Arabic appears to favor the African Demonic script.

HIEROGLYPHIC.	TRANSITION.	CHARACTER.	ANCIENT NAME.	MEANING.
		א		
		ב	בת Beth.	An House.
		ג	נאה Gah.	An Arm.
		ד	דע Dau.	The Lips.
		ה	הה Heh.	The Breath
		ו	וו Vav.	A Feather.

HIEROGLYPHIC.	TRANSITION.	CHARACTER.	ANCIENT NAME.	MEANING.
		ס	סאה SAH.	THE MOON.
		ע	עיל AUL.	THE LEGS.
		פ	פה PHEH.	THE FACE.
		צ	צי TZI.	A HORNED BEAST.
		ק	קאי KAV.	A BOAT.
		ש		
		ת	תאת THATH.	A TENT.

HIEROGLYPHIC.	TRANSITION.	CHARACTER.	ANCIENT NAME.	MEANING.
			זאן ZAN.	A KNIFE.
			חח CHACH.	THE BOSOM.
			טאה TAH.	A SPADE.
			אי AI.	THE EYE.
			כאה CAH.	A SLING.
			לי LI.	A LION.
			מם MIM.	WATER.
			נאה NAH.	A CUP.

99

Coptic and Greek Alphabet

Coptic	Greek	Name of	the Letter	English Sound	Number
Ⲁⲁ	Αα	Ⲁⲗⲫⲁ	Alpha	a	1
Ⲃⲃ	Ββ	Ⲃⲏⲧⲁ	Beta	b	2
Ⲅⲅ	Γγ	Ⲅⲁⲙⲙⲁ	Gamma	g	3
Ⲇⲇ	Δδ	Ⲇⲉⲗⲧⲁ	Delta	d	4
Ⲉⲉ	Εε	Ⲉⲓ	Ei	e (short)	5
Ⲍⲍ	Ζζ	Ⲍⲓⲧⲁ	Zita	z	7
Ⲏⲏ	Ηη	ⲉⲏⲧⲁ	Heta	a (long)	8
Ⲑⲑ	Θθ	Ⲑⲏⲧⲁ	Theta	th	9
Ⲓⲓ	Ιι	Ⲓⲱⲧⲁ	Iota	i	10
Ⲕⲕ	Κκ	Ⲕⲁⲡⲡⲁ	Kappa	k	20
ⲗλ	Λλ	ⲗⲁⲩⲇⲁ	Lauda	l	30
Ⲙμ	Μμ	Ⲙⲓ	Mi	m	40
Ⲛⲛ	Νν	Ⲛⲓ	Ni	n	50
Ⲝⲝ	Ξξ	Ⲝⲓ	Xi	x (ks)	60
Ⲟⲟ	Οο	Ⲟⲩ	Ou	o	70
Ⲡⲡ	Ππ	Ⲡⲓ	Pi	p	80
Ⲣⲣ	Ρρ	Ⲣⲟ	Ro	r	100
Ⲥⲥ	Σσ	Ⲥⲓⲙⲁ	Sima	s	200
Ⲧⲧ	Ττ	Ⲧⲁⲩ	Tau	t	300
Ⲩⲩ	Υυ	Ⲩⲉ	Ue	u	400
Ⲫⲫ	Φφ	Ⲫⲓ	Phi	ph	500
Ⲭⲭ	Χχ	Ⲭⲓ	Chi	kh	600
Ⲯⲯ	Ψψ	Ⲯⲓ	Psi	ps	700
Ⲱⲱ	Ωω	Ⲁⲩ	Au	oo (long)	800
Ϣϣ		Ϣⲉⲓ	Shei	sh	
Ϥϥ		Ϥⲉⲓ	Fei	f	90
Ϧϧ		Ϧⲉⲓ	Khei	ch, kh	
Ϩϩ		Ϩⲟⲣⲓ	Hori	h	900
Ϫϫ		Ϫⲁⲛϫⲓⲁ	Janjia	j, g	
Ϭϭ		Ϭⲓⲙⲁ	Gima	g, k, sk	
Ϯϯ		Ⲧⲉⲓ	Tei	ti, di, th	

ιαω ιουω· ιαω· αωι· ωια ψινωθερ· θερωψιν· ωψιθερ· νεφθομαωθ· νεφιομαωθ· μαραχαχθα· μαρμαραχθα· ιηαπα μεναμαν· αμαννι του ουρανου· ισραϊ ζαμην ζαμην· σουβαϊβαϊ· αππααπ· ζαμην· ζαμην· δεραδαϊ· ζαπαζου· ζαμην· ζαμην· σαρσαρτου· ζαμην· ζαμην· κουκιαμιν· μιαϊ· ζαμην· ζαμην· ιαϊ· ιαϊ· τουαπ· ζαμην· ζαμην· ζαμην· μαιν· μαρι· μαριν· μαρει· ζαμην· ζαμην· ζαμην

From top; Hieroglyphics, Demonic, Coptic

101

Bibliography

Black Man of the Nile and His Family, B. Jochannan, 1981

A Coptic Dictionary, W.E. Crum, Clarendon Press, 1939

Diodorus of Sicily, C.H Oldfather, Harvard University Press, 1968

Egyptian Book of the Dead, Budge, Dover Publication Inc., 1967

Egypt and the Old Testament, T. Eric Peet, African Publication Society, reprint 1983

Egyptian Language, Budge, Dover Publications Inc., 1976

Grammar of the Coptic Language, Black, G., 1893

Herodotus - The Histories, Penguin Books, 1966

Hieroglyphic Dictionary, 2 vol., Budge, Dover Publication, 1978

Introduction to African Civilization, Jackson, J.G, Citadel Press, 1970

Kemet and the African World View, University of Sankore Press, 1986

The Mummy, Budge, Dover Publication, 1989

Newsweek, January 11, 1988 "The Search for Adam and Eve"

Osiris, and the Egyptian Resurrection, vol 1, Budge, Dover Publication 1973

Stolen Legacy, George G.M. James, 1954

The Thirteenth Tribe, Koestler, A., Popular Library, 1978

U. B. & U. S. COMMUNICATIONS SYSTEMS

1040-D Settlers Landing Rd. .... 2601-B Chestnut Ave.
Hampton, Virginia 23669 .... Newport News, Virginia 23607
(804) 723-2696 .... (804) 380-9300

BOOKS WRITTEN BY THE HONORABLE ELIJAH MUHAMMAD

THE THEOLOGY OF TIME (available: April, 1992)

Hard back, Delux edition, Books 1, 2. 3 & 4 bound together	....
Paperback Edition, Books, 1, 2, 3 & 4 bound together	....
Book 1 (paper) "Knowledge of Allah and His Messenger"	....
Book 2 (paper) "Root of the Creation of the Blackman"	....
Book 3 (paper("The root of the Creation of the White Race" Knowledge of the Devil	....
Book 4 "The Judgement is Now!" Knowledge of this Day & Time	....
Message to the Blackman in America	$10.00
How To Eat to Live, Book One	8.95
How To Eat to Live, Book Two	9.95
Our Saviour Has Arrived	11.95
Fall of America	11.95
Supreme Wisdom, Book One	3.95
Supreme Wisdom, Book Two	5.95
The True History of Jesus	6.95

BOOKS WRITTEN ABOUT THE NATION OF ISLAM

The Legacy of The Honorable Elijah Muhammad	3.95
The Life and Teaching of Master Fard Muhammad, By Hakim Shabazz	$7.95
Master Fard Muhammad, Detroit History, Edited By Prince A. Cuba	3.95
Freedom Justice & Equality; Teachings of the Nation of Islam, By Greg Parks	4.95
Message to the White Man: Yakub and the Origins of White Supremacy	11.95
Seven Speeches By Minister Farrakhan	9.95
Holy Qur'an, By Maulana Ali	19.95

OTHER BOOKS PUBLISHED BY UBUSCS

Aspects of Euro-Centric Thought: Racism, Imperialism & Sexism, By Adib Rashad	13.95
The Power of Thought, By Kendryck V. Allen	8.95
Stolen Legacy, By George G. M. James	13.95
Profusion: Analysis of the Impact of The Blackman's Guide, By H. Khalif Khalifah	5.95
How To Publish & Distribute Your Own Newspaper, Magazine or Book, By H. Khalif Khalifah	3.95
100 Amazing Facts About The Negro, By J. A. Rogers	3.95
MUSA: A Story of Moses, By Prince A. Cuba	6.95
African Fables, By Dr. Linus A. Bassey	6.95
Basketball Jones, By Keith Kelly	3.95
Tribute to John G. Jackson, By Adib Rashad & H. Khalif Khalifah	3.95
Words From An Unchained Mind, By Steven Whitehurst	9.95
Putting It All Together, By Terrance Jackson	7.95
Struggle, By Shelomi	5.95
Blackl Exodus, By Neal Jackson	10.95
MisAdventures of Primordial Man, By Edgar Ridley	3.95
Capoeira: African Brazilian Karate, By Yusef Abdul Salaam	5.95
Hatshepsut: Black African Queen of the Nile, By Prof. John F. Hatchett	5.95
To The Woman, By Prince A. Cuba	2.95
Am I Asking Too Much, By Gwen Tait-Dover	6.95
How Beautiful De Swatches, By Marva Cooper	3.95
The Art of Dreadlocks, By Wanda M. Johnson	4.50